1995

JE ME SOUVIENS

A novel by
James R. Coggins

Mill Lake Books

Mill Lake Books
Abbotsford, BC
Canada
www.coggins.ca

Cover design by Dean Tjepkema

Printed by Lightning Source, distributed by Ingram

ISBN 978-0-9881462-7-3

1

YOU DO NOT REMEMBER, Pierre, how it was then. But me, I remember. You cannot remember, but I cannot forget.

How could you remember? You are young. You were not there. But I, Jean Tonnerre, was there. I saw everything. I heard the words, the speeches. I felt the emotions. I met the people. I experienced momentous events. I knew them all firsthand.

And Pierre Roche did too. Pierre was my good friend. You were born later, after it was all over, of course, but when you were born, I named you after my friend Pierre. Perhaps in you I hoped to keep a little of my friend alive, as well as myself. He is gone now. They are all gone except for me. I am the last, and I am an old man. Well, maybe not so very old in years, but the years have been hard, and I have seen a lot.

Pierre and I were not the only ones, you see. There were many who saw and experienced those phenomenal times, especially that exciting, pivotal year when so much happened. Just one year, and yet it changed everything. And the twelve of us were right at the heart of it all. We saw and experienced everything—I, Pierre, my brother Jacques and the others—the selection of the twelve of us, The Long March to Nowhere, The Time of Random Atrocities, The Unquenchable Fire, The Advance of the Tanks.

I have experienced a lot, and I know that few people have their dreams fulfilled. But we saw our dreams fulfilled, saw them fulfilled with our own eyes. No, it's more than that. We weren't just there. We were participants. We built our dream with our own hands. And when the fateful night came, we were there, right in the heart of the action, representatives of the dream, twelve witnesses of the new nation.

You are young. I had such hopes for you. That's what we did it for, so that things would be different for you. Well, they are different, though I'm not sure you would say they are better.

Yes, I understand you must leave soon, and there is not much time. No, don't worry about that. I don't think your namesake would be angry at you. Pierre would have understood. Our people have always understood—we dream with our hearts, but we use our heads to pay the bills.

Yes, Pierre, you are right. It is time I stopped talking in generalities and spoke about facts. I understand. You deal in hard, cold facts—or should I say hard, cold cash? And who could blame you? There is no future for a young man here now—at least, no economic future. You have to choose between your heart and your head, between your pride and your wallet. You need to put food in your stomach.

And that is what it was about, you know—that fateful choice which determined everything which has happened since. We insisted we had the right to choose—to choose between our hearts and our wallets. We haven't always chosen the same way, of course, but that time—to everyone's surprise—we chose our hearts.

2

YOU DO NOT UNDERSTAND, Pierre. How could you? Let me explain it to you from the beginning. I shall start by explaining how it was that we won the October 1995 referendum that separated Quebec from Canada.

Do not take for granted that that was inevitable, Pierre. No, no. In fact, when the referendum campaign began, it seemed inevitable that we would lose. As late as four weeks before the October 30 vote, we were six to ten percent behind in the polls.

The No side, those who wanted Quebec to remain in Canada—they said that the turning point came October 7, when Lucien Bouchard took over from Jacques Parizeau as leader of the Yes campaign. Or they made that spurious charge of "electoral irregularities." That was just an English lie. Or if there were some irregularities, they were certainly not enough to change the result—only enough to provide the English with an excuse to try to thwart the will of the people. The real people of Quebec, I mean, the Québécois. Not those who opposed us, the English and the ethnics and the bankers, who are no people.

Oh, it is true that in a few polling stations there were more ballots cast than there were registered voters, but I ask you: Was it not just that we voted for the disenfranchised—the dead, those who had been forced to move away, the babies who were not yet born, like you, Pierre? (That surely puts a different meaning on the old call for "la guerre des

5

bébés"![1]) And yes, it is true that there were a high number of No ballots rejected as spoiled ballots in some polls. But it does not matter. All of that can be explained by the "God factor."

In any case, those things may have had some effect, but they alone do not explain the decisiveness of the vote, the unexpectedly high margin of victory, the overwhelming majority that was at the same time the fulfilment of our highest hopes and the factor that forced everyone to accept the vote as irreversible. They alone do not explain how we managed to achieve a Yes vote of 79 percent, how it was that virtually every francophone in Quebec voted for separation.

No, I would place the turning point earlier, on September 30. That was the night that Normand LaChance was beaten to death outside a bar in North Bay, Ontario. He was a Québécois beaten to death by a mob of English bastards. He was a symbol of all the oppression that we Québécois have endured at the hands of the English for two and a half centuries.

The police investigation later claimed that he was only half-French—the English police, of course. His mother, in fact, had been real English, a war bride in the Second World War. The police also claimed that the fight didn't have anything to do with the fact that LaChance was French. He spoke English without an accent, and the men who beat him claimed they didn't know his name. The fight was about some girl in the bar, they said.

It didn't matter. He was a Québécois—well, it was reported that he had lived all of his life in North Bay, but the important thing was his blood. He had Québécois blood. He was a Québécois beaten to death by English bastards, and he represented all of the Québécois repeatedly oppressed and mistreated by generations of English. That was how we portrayed him. We used him in our brochures, in our ads, in our speeches and in our street corner conversations. Whatever else he may have been, he was a martyr, and he served us very well.

That was when the flag burnings began. Some drunk 20-year-old in a bar in Vancouver stood up and said that all the frogs should be beaten, and then he burned a Quebec flag right in the pub. It might not have been noticed, but it started a small fire. At least a couple of people were burned quite badly, and that gave it some attention. Soon people were burning Quebec flags in bars all across Canada. Soon after that, they

---

[1] "The war of babies" or "revenge of the cradle."

were burning flags out in the open, on legislature lawns, in public parks and in city plazas.

Oh, we burned a few Canadian flags, of course, but that was nothing new. We didn't burn that many. Well, we couldn't. There were hardly any Canadian flags in Quebec anyway. They were hard to find. We finally had to resort to stealing them from public buildings, from post offices and so on. It was hard. Some of the poles were pretty tall. Sometimes we just had to knock the whole pole down.

Then the English did something stupid. I blame them for making the situation much worse. They began trying to guard the flagpoles. So we had to get a bigger crowd of francophones to storm the flagpoles. Then shoving started, and, you know, one thing led to another. This happened in English Canada too, not just Quebec. And that's how some of the fighting started.

Altogether, we calculated one or two more people may have been killed, and others injured. Maybe dozens of them. Perhaps hundreds. You couldn't count them all. And that's just the Québécois. There might have been more if you count the English, which I don't.

Were the casualty counts real? Who knows? It wasn't always easy to determine what violence in Canadian society was due to the Quebec question and what had other causes. We just collected what statistics and examples we could. They were useful, and that's all that matters.

Those figures don't include that final rally in Montreal, of course. That was another stupid move on the part of the English, and it was clearly against the referendum rules. The rules said clearly that it was only the Québécois who had a right to decide the future of Quebec, no one else. But those stubborn English decided to butt in. On the last weekend before the referendum vote, they decided to have a mass rally in Montreal. They flew in thousands of people from all over Canada—at the expense of the Canadian government and big businesses that were afraid their profits might be hurt by separation.

Imagine it—a hundred and fifty thousand English invading downtown Montreal. They got off the buses and staged a huge rally. It was inevitable that that would lead to trouble. After the rally, the hundred and fifty thousand fanned out across the city, looking for Québécois. They began by talking, urging Québécois to stay in Canada. Then a flag was burned. The talking turned to arguing, the arguing turned to pushing, and in the middle of the pushing a punch was thrown, a knife was pulled....

The result was chaos. A running battle went on all night. The police were called out, but it wasn't clear whether they were trying to stop the fighting or take part in it. No one knows how many were killed, how many were injured. Afterward, everyone was too preoccupied with other things to count. Events overtook the riot. It tipped the balance irretrievably to the Yes side—after that, no one would vote for the hated English. Once the vote had been taken, the riot no longer mattered. Looking back, it seems a minor skirmish, but it was a portent of much worse to come.

There was one other thing I want to relate to you. I was there. My brother Jacques and I were there. We were in the thick of the arguing. We didn't know for sure at that point if we would win the referendum, and we were still doing everything we could to make it happen. Yes, I was part of the arguing. And the other? Don't ask me that, Pierre. Well, it was a long time ago. Who remembers what one might have done, what in fact one did? I'm sure I did nothing that I could be ashamed of. Everything I was doing, I did to help my country.

But there was something else I wanted to tell you. At one point, in the middle of the riot in Montreal, an old man grabbed me by the jacket. I thought he was going to strike me, but instead he spoke to me. He was dressed in a long white T-shirt that hung down to his knees over his blue jeans. He had long white hair and a long white beard. He was obviously English because he spoke French with a bad accent and a limited vocabulary. But his words struck me. He struck me with his words. In the middle of that surging, pushing mob, he said:

"Je veux, je dois vous dire une leçon de l'histoire. Écoutez. Il y a beaucoup des années, plus d'un siècle, et c'était loin d'ici, a l'ouest. Un fou a tué un homme stupide. C'est triste, mais c'est réalité. Mais le fou était français, et l'homme stupide était anglais. Alors, tous les anglais ont défendu l'homme stupide. Et tous les français ont défendu le fou. Pourquoi? Je pense, moi, que tous les anglais étaient fous, tous les français étaient stupides, tous les canadiens étaient fous et stupides. Nous devons apprendre à juger avec sagacité. Nous devons apprendre à juger par sagacité."[2]

_____

[2] "I want, I must tell you a lesson from history. Listen. Many years ago, more than a century, and far from here, in the west, a madman killed a stupid man. It was sad, but it happened. But the madman was French, and the stupid man was

Then he let me go and was gone into the crowd. I caught sight of him once or twice, grabbing now one, now another, telling them his story, then moving on. I often think of that man and wonder if his words were prophetic.

CALM RETURNED in the morning, but after that night it was clear what the result would be. We knew that we had won. My brother Jacques and I were no longer needed in Montreal. None of the Yes workers were needed any more. We no longer needed to work or fight. The battle was over.

Monsieur Bouchard knew that too. That was why he called me and Jacques to join him in Quebec City. Out of all of the Yes workers, he selected twelve of us, twelve young men, to represent the Québécois of the future, to represent the new nation of Quebec. We were honoured, I can tell you. I already knew my friend Pierre Roche, of course, and his brother André and a couple of others, but that was when I met the rest of Monsieur Bouchard's other young followers.

Pierre and André and Jacques and I were from upper middle class families. Our parents actually owned a number of fishing boats and a processing factory in eastern Quebec, Roche et Tonnerre Lte. Yes, Pierre, in those days we had money. It is hard to think of it now, but we were quite comfortable then. Pierre and Jacques and I had come to Montreal to study at the university. Yes, Pierre, in those days there were many universities—French-speaking universities—and we could afford to go there. Anyway, that is where we became involved in the Separatist movement, and during the referendum campaign Jacques and I were assigned to work in Montreal.

The other eight? Philippe Batisse was from the same region of Quebec as we were, although we had not met him before. He had a friend named Nathan Thomson, who was a lawyer in the eastern townships, where we had grown up, but he was not from there originally.

Then there was Thomas Didime. Thomas, well, let us say that

English. Therefore, all the English defended the stupid man. And all the French defended the madman. Why? I think that all the English were mad, all the French were stupid, all the Canadians were mad and stupid. We must learn to judge with wisdom. We must learn to judge by wisdom."

Thomas was sometimes confused. We did not know that till later, of course. He had a twin brother who was a strong federalist, a strong proponent of Quebec remaining in Canada, and I think that affected him a great deal. He had been assigned to work in eastern Quebec.

Matthieu Levis was an accountant who worked in the tax department of the Canadian government. That's right, Pierre, the Canadian government. Oh, I know they teach you nowadays in school that we Québécois were shut out from jobs in the Canadian government, but that is an exaggeration. There were some who did get jobs there, a few. After all, they needed someone who understood French and could collect English taxes from the Québécois.

How could he work on the referendum campaign? Pierre, you ask such questions. He took holiday time, a vacation. I think his supervisor knew what he was doing. Was he allowed? Well, how could they stop him? It was a free country. You must not try to read the current situation back into the past. What we have now is a temporary aberration due to the difficult circumstances we find ourselves in. Things were different then. It is hard to explain, but perhaps when I have finished my story, you will understand.

Then there were Jacques Petit and Judas de Coeur and Simon Rose. Simon came from a family that had been involved in the first attempts to gain Quebec's independence back in the 1960s, the Front de Libération du Québec. The FLQ had blown up a few Canada Post mailboxes, symbols of the English oppression. And they had kidnapped and killed a couple of people. Nothing very major. I think Monsieur Bouchard chose him to be among the twelve of us for symbolic reasons. He provided continuity, a sense of history, tradition. The Rose name had great prestige in Quebec in those days because of the oppression his family had suffered. Yes, they had been in prison. Several years in prison for the life of an English dog—it was a gross injustice. Pierre, you ask such strange questions. No, they were not executed. Canada had abolished capital punishment in those days. It seems strange to think of now. In any case, the English sent the army in, and crushed the FLQ. It was a terribly dark and oppressive time.

Oh, yes, the twelfth. The twelfth was Judas Simon d'Estaing. We didn't know much about him at the time, and what I know now is best forgotten. He worked for a bank. He was assigned to raise money for the referendum, and I was told he did a very good job. I was also told that he had kept some of the money for himself. I believe that, though I have no proof. But I knew him, and I believe it.

OH, BUT THAT WAS an exciting evening, Pierre! You should have seen it. We were confident of victory by then, but none of us had anticipated the sheer magnitude of it. And when Monsieur Bouchard and Jacques Parizeau made their victory speeches, we were right there. They gathered us around them, symbols of the new Quebec, the brightest and best that Quebec had to offer, symbols of the future. And we cheered. As loyal followers, we cheered these messiahs who had led our nation into the promised land of national sovereignty. We cheered everything that night. Even when Monsieur Parizeau declared victory over "money and the ethnic vote," pouring contempt on those that had voted No. "We will have our own country, and we will have our own revenge!" he shouted. We responded with chants of "Le Québec aux Québécois!"[3]

We did not know then how those words would be received, how some would put them into practice. No matter. They were true words, and one should always speak truth, no matter what the consequences. They were the words in our hearts, and our hearts were full of triumph.

How could we know that some would take those words literally, that some Québécois youths would take to the streets in Montreal and beat up any ethnics that they saw? We are responsible for the words we speak, of course, but we are not responsible for what others do with them. Monsieur Parizeau did not tell the youths to go and do what they did. The problem, of course, is that it was too late in some areas. The Québécois youth were outnumbered, overwhelmed by the ethnic hordes that had almost swamped our dream of a nation. Almost, but not quite. In the end, it was not so much revenge as a running street battle between Québécois and ethnics, Québécois and English, police and anybody who happened to be there.

"Money" was also not overlooked. The youths smashed windows and looted stores all down St. Catherine Street. A few places were burned. Any place with an English sign, no matter how small, was a target. The store owners had asked for this, of course. In trying to thwart the will of the people, they incurred the inevitable consequences. You always pay for injustice.

Most of the No supporters stayed in the No headquarters in Montreal overnight, and that was wise. A few tried to leave and suffered

---

[3] "Quebec for Quebeckers!"

the consequences. Later, this incident was overblown. Windows were broken in the headquarters, but most of the No supporters escaped unhurt simply by staying inside. How could they show their cowardly faces after the defeat they had suffered?

Later, there was confusion about what damage had been caused by the post-referendum riots, what had been caused earlier in the post-rally riots and what was caused later. It was an argument for insurance companies perhaps, but none of them are headquartered in Quebec, and in the end they did not pay. No wonder. The insurance companies were run by English bastards, and they did not even take care of their own.

The damage and the rioting do not matter, in any case. They distract attention from the significant event. On October 30, 1995, the Québécois people freed themselves from chains that had bound them for two and a half centuries. They declared their freedom. They voted themselves into existence as a new nation, proud, independent and full of potential.

3

POTENTIAL. I have seen much, Pierre, and I have learned that you cannot tell what the future holds—yours now or ours then. The new Quebec was full of potential, brand new, like each of us when we are born, like the world when it was first created. Almost anything was possible. As events proved, Quebec had potential that we had not even dreamed of. But there are many kinds of potential, Pierre. There can be potential for evil as well as potential for good. We had forgotten the history of the Garden of Eden when we tried to create the Garden of Quebec. There was much potential in the new Quebec for good and for evil, and who could know what would be fulfilled? Many things could have happened in the new Quebec, Pierre, but I will tell you about the things that did happen.

We had won the referendum, so you might suppose that separation followed as a matter of course. Things were not quite so simple. They never are. You see, the referendum question called for Quebec to become sovereign only after Quebec made a "formal offer to Canada for a new economic and political partnership."

Yes, Pierre, that sounds pretty confusing. Why didn't we offer the people a clearer question? Because we would have lost, of course. The point was that we had to get a Yes answer to the question, any question, and then we could do what we wanted.

Some people assumed that we really wanted to remain part of Canada and were only using the threat of separation to get a better deal.

Even some Yes voters thought that, maybe even many Yes voters, and our leaders had as good as promised those people that they would have another chance later to vote on whatever deal was worked out or they could vote to accept separation if no deal could be reached.

Of course, nobody had planned for a 79 percent vote. Our leaders had made careful plans, and the government of France was ready to recognize Quebec as an independent country, but our leaders had expected to have to move carefully, to have to negotiate each step, to have to manage public opinion very carefully. All that became unnecessary, but this caught our leaders by surprise. They were not ready to simply declare independence right away.

After a day or two to celebrate and to let the victory sink in, Monsieur Parizeau and Monsieur Bouchard made an offer to the government of Canada to begin negotiations on separation. Their negotiating position was quite simple. They wanted a separate country. Quebec would take over all of the federal assets in Quebec, military bases, post offices, bank accounts, everything. The Quebec government would take over any Canadian government debts owed to Québécois, and the Canadian government would be responsible for the rest. We would continue to use the Canadian dollar, and Quebec-based companies could continue to do business in Canada. The railways and highways and the St. Lawrence Seaway would remain in place, with Quebec gaining ownership of those sections that were inside Quebec. Canadian tax laws would be operative till the end of the fiscal year, and then be replaced by Quebec laws and social programs—the details all to be negotiated, of course. All along, we had expected to have to negotiate separation, but in the end there proved to be nothing to negotiate, and no one to negotiate with.

There was no reply to the Quebec government's offer. The government of Canada had actually made some secret plans for what to do in the event of a Yes vote, but they were made with the expectation of a close vote that might be reversed if the right concessions were made. They didn't know what to do with a 79 percent vote. The referendum of October 30 thrust the Canadian government into a crisis that left it paralyzed for almost a month. There was a lot of babbling in the English press, but for the most part our victory was greeted in English Canada by a stunned silence. No one was sure what to say or do, the Canadian government most of all.

Governments think they can control events they set in motion, but they cannot. Governments are not God. They are not that powerful. In 1969, when the Canadian government legalized abortion but only if the mother's life or health was in danger, the prime minister did not say that that would lead within a few years to over one hundred thousand abortions every year, virtually abortion on demand. And when the same prime minister eased divorce regulations so that people would not be forced to stay in hopeless marriages, he did not say that one-third to one-half of all marriages would turn out to be hopeless or that it would mean that there would be a million and a half single mothers living in poverty in Canada. No, he did not say those things, but perhaps he should have. If he was as wise as he claimed to be, he should have known. There comes a time in every revolution when those who start the revolution lose control to others who are more radical. Once you have removed the chains, it is hard to fit the dog with a longer leash.

This is what happened in the new Quebec, Pierre. The governments lost control of events—and it was one of us who set things moving—and incidentally who finally jerked the Canadian government out of its paralysis.

Matthieu Levis had an uncle named Simon Levis who owned a factory making parts for television sets. No, Pierre, not just television sets for the English—for us as well. Almost every one of us had a television set in those days. Some people had two or three. And there were French-language TV stations to watch on them, too.

Yes, Pierre, it is hard to understand these things, but no matter. It is enough that you understand that Matthieu's Uncle Simon owned a factory, with a couple of hundred workers. It was not a large factory, but it was not a small one either.

Simon and his nephew Matthieu got together to discuss Canadian government taxes—Matthieu worked for Revenue Canada, the Canadian government taxation department, remember—and together they came up with a radical plan. Matthieu did not consult with Monsieur Bouchard or Monsieur Parizeau, the men who had proclaimed him a representative of the new Quebec. The two Levis acted on their own.

Exactly two weeks after the referendum, on November 13, Simon Levis called a press conference. Everyone was calling press conferences in those days, but Simon's attracted some attention. It didn't hurt that his nephew Matthieu was there, an employee of Revenue Canada. There were not a lot of reporters there, but three or four were enough to get the word out on what Simon was planning. Simon announced that, effective immediately, he would pay no more taxes to the Canadian government. The income tax he had collected from his employees, their unemployment insurance deductions, the tax on his business profits, his personal income taxes—all of it. He simply refused to pay. He said he would still withhold these taxes and deductions from his employees' paycheques but that, rather than sending them to Ottawa, he would keep them—in trust for the new Quebec national government, of course. He did that, though I am not sure that the Quebec government ever received any of the money.

Matthieu told me later that his uncle was on the verge of bankruptcy. He actually hadn't paid any taxes or forwarded money to Ottawa for some months. So, I suppose Simon's motive may have been just to save his own company from bankruptcy. But our actions always have implications beyond our own lives.

The Canadian government could get along without Simon's taxes. The government had been getting along without them for some months anyway. But Simon's action set a precedent. It was the first pebble that fell, and it triggered a great avalanche. The next day, as soon as word got out, no less than fifty-two other companies and individuals called press conferences to announce that they, too, would no longer pay taxes to the Canadian government. The press went to the first few press conferences, but they soon gave up. It was too much. When everyone gets publicity, no one gets any.

The day after that, another three hundred and twenty-one businesses and individuals joined the growing movement. One of the Montreal newspapers took the trouble to make an accurate count. There was euphoria. People were cheering in the streets. It was a tax holiday of gargantuan proportions. In fact, some people also refused to pay taxes to the Quebec government—they were mostly English and ethnic bastards from Montreal. And some people refused to pay taxes to any government, including some English Canadians from Alberta and British Columbia, taking the position that it was unclear which governments were really legitimate and they would wait until things were clearer before paying any more taxes to anyone.

The government of Quebec was not happy about this. They did not want people to stop paying taxes; they just wanted all the taxes to go to the Quebec government. At first, Monsieur Parizeau and Monsieur Bouchard tried to downplay the significance of Simon Levis's actions.

16

They called for calm and order. They called for observance of the laws, and for people to wait until the government had formulated a plan for the transfer of tax monies.

On the fourth day, the Quebec government set up bank accounts in credit unions throughout Quebec and then made an announcement asking those who were refusing to pay their Canadian taxes to deposit an equivalent amount in these bank accounts. They promised that the credit unions would keep track of how much money each citizen had deposited.

A week later, on November 23, the Quebec national assembly passed a resolution calling for an end to "unjust taxation of Quebec citizens by foreign powers." It was a resolution which did not mean much. It did not actually counsel Québécois to refuse to pay Canadian taxes. It was equally compatible with the Quebec government's original position that the transfer of taxes and powers from the Canadian government to the Quebec government should be negotiated in an orderly manner. It was an attempt to save face. The Quebec government was trying to make it appear that refusing to pay taxes to Canada had been its idea—people were still lining up daily to announce that they, too, would not pay. It was rather silly really. The Quebec government was trying to pretend that it had not lost control of events, but it had. Yes, Pierre, the government leaders were not being truthful, but appearance and power matter more in politics than truth does. Governments may decide what is truth, Pierre, but governments do not control the world, not even Quebec governments.

By the end of the month, it became clear that very little money was making its way into the Quebec government bank accounts. The government made one more attempt and declared that funds deposited would be considered a loan to the new national government and would be repaid once the new Quebec was firmly established and prospering. I think the government hoped it would at least get to keep the money a while and earn interest on it. But it was a vain hope. Very little money ever came in, and by then no one cared about it anymore. There were far bigger issues to be concerned about.

ONE THING that Simon Levis's actions accomplished. If the government of Quebec was slow to respond, those actions finally stirred the government of Canada into action. It was like a huge monster awakening out of hibernation. On the day after the referendum, the

Canadian government had adjourned Parliament. Now, early on the morning of November 27, Prime Minister Chretien called the Canadian Parliament back into session. Yes, Pierre, I said Chretien. Jean Chretien was the prime minister. You find it remarkable that a Québécois could get elected prime minister? Then you would find it more remarkable that in fact a Québécois was prime minister for almost all of the last twenty-six years of Canada's united existence. How was that possible for an oppressed people? It is difficult to explain, but Chretien was a traitor to his people, a puppet of the English majority. Yes, yes, and the prime ministers before him were puppets too.

Don't ask useless questions, Pierre. I was telling you about the government of Canada. It will tell you something of what kind of a man Jean Chretien was that, early on the morning of November 27, he called Parliament back into session—without informing most of the Quebec Members of Parliament. Yes. Pierre, Quebec had Members of Parliament just like the rest of Canada, and most of them were convinced separatists, members of the Bloc Québécois, a party whose stated goal was to take Quebec out of Canada. Why did the English allow this, Pierre? That is a good question. Myself, I think it is because the English were stupid. That and the fact that the English believed in democracy, in free speech, freedom of association, human rights—a whole host of ideas that are difficult to explain to you now. I tell you, you mustn't let the current conditions mislead you. They are only a temporary expedient due to the difficult situation we find ourselves in. Quebec will also have democracy and freedom some day. Soon, Pierre, soon.

There was also fear. You asked why the English allowed separatists to speak and write and get elected to Parliament. It was partly fear, Pierre. The English were afraid that if they tried to clamp down on the Separatists, if they started arresting or shooting our people, they would drive more Québécois into becoming Separatists. And they were probably right. But once the Québécois had voted Yes in the referendum, once all the Québécois were already Separatists, then there was nothing left to fear. And then the English acted. It was too late, but they acted. And they acted with a harshness and a decisiveness that must have surprised even themselves.

That bastard Chretien called Parliament back into session in the early morning of November 27. The first thing Parliament did was to pass a bill depriving all of the Quebec Members of Parliament of their seats. They passed it, first, second and third reading, inside an hour. And the governor-general, that puppet of the English queen, was waiting in the corridor to sign it into law. That was not legal, Pierre. It was a violation of the Canadian Constitution and the Canadian Charter of Rights and Freedoms. It was a violation of English principles. But laws do not control governments, Pierre. Governments make laws. And power controls governments. So power is law.

Then, the Canadian government passed a whole series of laws, tens of them in one day, hundreds in a week. A government that took years to decide on the colour of a flag, made fundamental changes without even reading the legislation. Whatever the government proposed, the Members of Parliament approved. It was a frenzy, Pierre. Of course, the other MPs knew that they could be removed just as the Québécois MPs had been, so they were wise enough not to ask too many questions.

The second law removed the Quebec judges from the Canadian Supreme Court; more than that, it removed Quebec justice from the Supreme Court. That meant that whatever laws the Canadian government passed would not be overturned by the Supreme Court.

The salaries for the Quebec MPs and their pensions were stopped. The Canadian government also stopped all money from being sent to Quebec—pensions, disability cheques, unemployment insurance payments, paycheques to government employees, child tax credits, grants to the Quebec government. Yes, yes, Pierre, the Canadian government gave money to Quebec citizens, lots of it, and to the Quebec government as well. I know they teach you nowadays that the Canadian government just took money out of Quebec and never sent any back, but that is not exactly true. Many of the Canadian government programs were universal—they went to every citizen, whether English, ethnic or Québécois. In fact, sometimes, the Canadian government was even accused of favouritism, of giving programs and concessions to Quebec in order to bribe us into wanting to stay in Canada. But that is just an English lie, of course. We all know that Canada took more money out of Quebec than it put back in.

It doesn't matter, Pierre. That is far in the past. What matters is that on November 27, 1995, the Canadian government ceased paying any money at all to Québécois. Well, to almost all Québécois. The Quebec MPs in the Liberal Party, including that bastard Chretien, were all hired as "advisors" to the new Canadian government.

I think they did this as a last-ditch attempt to convince Québécois

19

how much they would lose if they were to separate from Canada. It did not work. What it actually meant was that at that moment the Canadian government ceased to exercise any authority in Quebec. The Canadian government had recognized that Quebec was now an independent country!

A cabinet minister named Lloyd Axworthy was made the new prime minister, although we suspected that Chretien and the other Quebec cabinet ministers were still telling him what to do. There were rumours they still attended cabinet meetings. Of course, there were many rumours in those days.

It was the Quebec government that went into shock then. All of its work had been geared toward separation, and now that separation had been handed to us, the Quebec government didn't know what to do. It didn't actually have plans for how it would govern the new nation.

It was the middle of December before the Quebec government took action itself. Then, on December 15, it expelled all of the members of the Quebec National Assembly who were not members of the Parti Québécois—all of the rich English bastards from Montreal and the lower class ethnics. Oh, there were a few Québécois Liberals in the National Assembly, but they were all traitors, like that bastard Chretien—and they got what they deserved. The Quebec government filled the vacancies with the Bloc Québécois MPs who had been unjustly deprived of their positions in the Canadian Parliament—gave them salaries and all. It was only fair. The new National Assembly now contained all of the leaders of the Separatist movement, all the true leaders of the true Québécois people.

The flaw, if there was one, was that the law the National Assembly passed to bring this about was drafted rather hastily, without second thought—as many laws were, on both sides, in those days. The new law did not specify how Members of the National Assembly would be elected in future. It would be a shame to deprive any of those noble men and women of their positions just because they happened to come from the same city or town as a member of the Parti Québécois. As well, the Parti Québécois had been elected two years earlier, but the Bloc members had just been appointed. When did their terms expire? No one knew. Would future Members of the National Assembly be elected—or just appointed as the true representatives of the true Québécois people? Again, no one knew. Democracy has its weaknesses, Pierre. You can't always guarantee the right people will be elected. That hastily drafted law is still in effect—right down to the present. I don't think those who drafted it had expected it to be in force for so long. They were thinking only of the present problem. We often do that, Pierre—underestimate the long-term effects of our simplest actions.

Of course, no one thought of that then. We were all too busy. There was too much to do. On December 20, the new National Assembly passed a Declaration of Sovereignty, to take effect January 1, 1996. What of the promise to put separation to a new vote if negotiations failed? That did not matter now. No one even thought of it or expected it. It did not matter. The new nation of Quebec had become a reality. The new nation was recognized immediately by the government of France, although other nations were slower to accept reality.

Remember this, Pierre, whatever others tell you. It was the declaration of the Quebec National Assembly that created the new nation of Quebec, not the presumptuous actions of the illegal government of Canada in November. That could not be. It was Quebec that was the new nation, and we could not be created by someone else's actions. We could not allow that. We were masters of our own destiny. We had to be.

4

THE WEST has never understood us. You understand, Pierre, when I talk of the West, I mean all of Canada west of the Quebec-Ontario border.

Ontario was the Canadian province closest to Quebec, and the people of Ontario always thought that they were our friends, that of all Canadians they understood us the best, that they were the ones who worked hardest to accommodate us. It is all nonsense, of course.

That attitude was an historical anomaly, Pierre. It dates back to the 1840s, when what was called Canada had only two parts, Upper Canada and Lower Canada, Ontario and Quebec. They had about equal population, but things were not equal, Pierre. That is why they called Ontario Upper Canada; they always wanted to partner with us—as long as they were on top.

The people of Ontario for a long while talked of Canada's two founding peoples, English and French. They were thinking of Ontario and Quebec—as if the Maritimes and the Prairies and British Columbia did not exist. They did exist, but Ontario believed that they existed only to be exploited by the people of Ontario. In the end, Ontario made sure that the Prairies became like Ontario. At the beginning, there were French and English on the Prairies—in fact, the French were there long before the English—but the English outlawed the French language, and drove the French off the land. That is why the Prairies and British Columbia are just exactly like Ontario, English fortresses. There are no

23

differences.

When people in Ontario say "West," they think of the Prairies and perhaps British Columbia. Or sometimes they think of Western civilization—that broad culture supposedly dominated by people of western European background and in fact dominated by those who speak English—if you can call that civilization, and I certainly don't. We are French, Pierre. We are not part of the West, not any more, certainly.

That is also why the rich English bastards in Montreal retreated to the western side of the city and called it Westmount. They may have lived in Quebec, but their hearts lived in the West. When we Québécois said "English," we meant all English Canadians, but we thought of the people of Westmount. The picture in our minds was of those rich English bastards in Montreal who oppressed us, who looked down their English noses at us and made it a point of pride never to learn the language of the people who surrounded them and worked for them and made them rich. The closer they were to Quebec, the more English and Western they were—and we hated them all, Pierre, hated them all with a passion.

I TOLD YOU, Pierre, that on November 27 the Canadian government suddenly stopped payments to all Québécois, pensions, unemployment insurance payments, paycheques, everything. I also told you that on December 20 the government of Quebec had declared independence as of January 1. But before that happened, on December 18, when we got up in the morning, there were guards—police and soldiers—on every bridge across the Ottawa River, and there were armed soldiers around all the government buildings in Hull. I can tell you, Pierre, there was a great outcry then, a lot of outrage and anger. That morning, when the thousands of Québécois who worked for the Canadian government—yes, yes, Pierre, I said thousands. Well, some of them were English who happened to live in Quebec because the houses were less expensive, but many of them were Québécois. The Canadian government had rules that many of its employees had to be bilingual, had to know English and French, and that eliminated a lot of English who were too stupid or too proud to learn French. There were thousands of Québécois who worked for the government of Canada, tens of thousands altogether. I don't care what they tell you in Quebec schools now, Pierre. I'm telling you how things really were.

Anyway, when the thousands of Québécois got in their cars

and—yes, Pierre, cars. Most people had cars in those days, one or two per family. Yes, Québécois as well as the English. I know we have very few cars now, Pierre, but we had them then. Pierre, I am never going to finish my story if you keep interrupting me with your questions.

So when the Québécois tried to drive across the bridges to get to their jobs in Ottawa or go to their jobs in government buildings in Hull, they were turned away with rifles and tanks. They were very angry. There was a big furore, I can tell you. You may think that was a foolish move, Pierre, because it antagonized the very Québécois who might be most favourable to staying part of Canada. But the Canadian government could no longer trust its employees. The government was afraid the employees would sabotage the workings of government and undermine and disrupt the work of the other employees. There *had* been one or two incidents—well, maybe more than that—no one knows for sure. To cite one example, the Canadian government claimed that a Québécois employee had sabotaged its child tax credit computer lists, deleting the names so that no Canadian would receive the cheques. Millions of Canadians were suddenly deprived of money they had been expecting. The back-up copies of the lists also disappeared about the same time. It is true that it was only the lists for those who filed their tax returns in English that were deleted—the lists for those who filed in French remained intact—but that was just a coincidence, an oddity of a computer glitch. I think that it was just an excuse and that the computers were deliberately sabotaged by the Canadian government in order to make Québécois look bad and to justify the harsh actions the government was taking against Québécois. I think the government also just wanted to keep the money. The financial crisis was just beginning. In any case, the lists were never restored, or at least the cheques were never issued again, even though it was two years before the Canadian government passed a law officially ending the tax credits.

I was saying it seemed a foolish move, Pierre, to close the border like that. But the Canadian government knew what it was doing. They had a plan, I'll concede that—an evil, cold-blooded plan. Five days later, when the outcry was at its height, the Canadian government announced that if any town or municipality in Quebec voted to become part of Canada again, then payments to its citizens would begin again, and the citizens could return to their Canadian government jobs if they had them.

It was a clever, evil plan, made without concern for human life. We had always maintained, Pierre, that the borders of Quebec were inviolable, that when a majority of Québécois voted to leave Canada, all of Quebec would leave Canada. We were one people, and we would remain that way.

But that clever, diabolical scheme worked, Pierre. It was the first attempt to change the borders of Quebec. Within three days, thirteen municipalities had voted to rejoin Canada after Quebec separated. Yes, it seems strange, because all but one or two of them had actually voted Yes in the referendum. But there were traitors, English spies in control of some of those towns.

You also have to understand that people's livelihoods were at stake. They became afraid, Pierre. It was one thing to vote with your heart to fulfil your dream of having your own country. It was quite another when your head told you that your wife and family might starve if you didn't have access to paycheques and unemployment cheques. The Quebec government responded that they would pay all the workers and pensioners from their own funds, but it was an empty promise. By then, everyone suspected they no longer had enough money to do that.

As I said, thirteen municipalities voted to rejoin Canada within three days, and others soon followed—perhaps forty or fifty in all, no one is really sure. Some voted to split in half, with half going each way. There was a lot of chaos really. Some Québécois began moving into the municipalities that had voted to rejoin Canada; many more I'm sure moved back to municipalities that were loyal to Quebec. There were even several thousand Québécois living in northern Ontario who moved back to Quebec. Yes, Pierre, there were Québécois in Ontario, especially in northern Ontario. Yes, Pierre, they had been allowed to keep the French language. There were even schools that taught in French, every subject in French. Well, yes, funded by the Ontario government—they were regular schools. Many of these people became afraid, afraid that they would lose their French schools now, afraid that they might be beaten and killed like Normand LaChance had been in North Bay. Anyway, these Québécois from Ontario moved back into Quebec, western Quebec, where many of the towns were voting to rejoin Canada. Some of them stopped there to try to change the vote, and some were forced to stop there when they ran out of gas or got caught up in the violence. It was chaos, and the strange thing is many of those municipalities never saw any of the cheques or the jobs the Canadian government said it was offering. It soon became evident it didn't have the money either.

Not all of the municipalities were in the west of Quebec. Some were farther east, surrounded by municipalities that chose to stay part of Quebec. And many of the votes had been close. It was an evil thing the Canadian government did in trying to change the borders of Quebec. It brought much evil.

OF ALL THE EVIL it brought, this for me this was the worst. My brother Jacques Tonnere was sent by the Quebec government to western Quebec to try to convince the municipalities not to separate but to remain part of Quebec. On January 15, he and his delegation came to a small town near the Ottawa River called Ville de Samaria. It was a town composed of a mixed race of people, some English, some Québécois. Jacques and his companions tried to see the mayor. The mayor refused to talk to them, and they were told to leave the town immediately. The town refused to even listen to Jacques and his delegation. Jacques was very angry, and he resolved to make an example of them. He phoned me and told me what he was going to do, and I agreed with him. He and his friends went to the next town and bought cans of gasoline and some matches. Late that night, they crept back into Ville de Samaria, determined to burn it to the ground. This would be one town that would not fall into the hands of the English.

But he was betrayed, Pierre. Armed men were waiting for him and his friends. There was some shooting, and Jacques was captured. Then the people of that town did a terrible thing, Pierre. They took Jacques to the nearest bridge over the Ottawa River, and they handed him over to the English. Jacques was taken to a prison in Ontario, where he was beaten and tortured. They went through the motions of a trial; it lasted two hours, and there was no one to defend him. Then, only three weeks after they had arrested him, on February 7, they executed him.

He was the first person to be executed in Canada in over thirty years. Canada had abolished the death penalty in the 1960s, but in that flurry of laws they passed in late 1995, Prime Minister Lloyd Axworthy's illegitimate Parliament brought back the death penalty—not just for treason, but for many offenses, fifteen specific crimes in fact, later expanded to twenty-three. They were saying they would show no tolerance to Québécois who broke their English laws. But it wasn't just Québécois. The new Canada was much less tolerant in general. One hundred and ninety-eight people were legally executed by the Canadian government in 1996, most of them English.

More than that, Jacques was also the first of us twelve young leaders, the twelve young apostles of the new Quebec, to die. It was a shock. He was dead before I even knew there had been a trial. It was then that I knew for sure that things would not turn out exactly as we had hoped. He was my brother, Pierre, and I loved him, and he was dead.

He was not the last.

THAT WAS WHEN the "Time of Random Atrocities" began. An English Canadian who lived in Hull and worked in Ottawa—I don't even think he worked for the government—was found stabbed to death in his apartment on the morning of February 8. Who knows? It may have been just a thief, or a disgruntled lover. But it was a snowflake that started another avalanche.

The next morning, two Québécois men were found dead in the same apartment building. The day after that, twelve people were found dead, in five different municipalities.

It was a terrible time, Pierre. People in a town would wake up each morning and find that another man or his family had been killed by his neighbours. It happened from both sides. The worst was a family of thirteen, found lined up on their front lawn, from the youngest to the oldest, with their throats slit. No one knew which side did it. Perhaps both sides had done it, just for practice. But whoever lined those children up must have known them, because they were lined up in order of age, not of height. Thousands of people died in this way.

THE CANADIAN GOVERNMENT'S STRATEGY worked, Pierre— to a point. Many municipalities in western Quebec voted to return to being part of Canada—but at a terrible cost. There was much anger, and anger turned to violence.

My good friend, whom you are named after, Pierre Roche, was there. He saw Quebec being torn apart by violence and knew the blame belonged to the Canadian government in Ottawa—and yet Ottawa was virtually untouched by the violence. It was not just. Pierre always had a passion for justice.

The result was that on the night of April 4, Pierre, Simon Rose and a few other Québécois slipped across the Ottawa River and entered the capital. I do not know what their plans were. The Canadian government later said that it was a well-organized plot to blow up the Parliament buildings. I don't know. What I do know is that they were surprised in a garden by some Canadian soldiers. There was some fighting. The soldiers seized Simon Rose. Pierre tried to free him. In the struggle he seized a rifle and tried to bayonet one of the soldiers, but only succeeded in slashing him across the side of his head, cutting off an ear.

Was it a plan to blow up the Parliament buildings? I do not know. They had some explosives with them, I do know that. And what if they did plan to blow up Parliament? Those bastards in Ottawa deserved to be blown up, after all the suffering they had caused.

Simon Rose died the next morning, of injuries he had received in the fighting. Rumours circulated that he had been beaten to death in his cell overnight.

There was another trial, this time a very public one in Ottawa. I think the Canadian government planned it that way, for propaganda purposes. After the trial, Pierre was also executed, publicly. It was April 30. They hung him, upside down, from a great scaffold that had been erected in front of the Parliament buildings, and then dropped a two-hundred-pound weight on a fifteen-foot rope tied around his neck. It tore his head off. No one asked whether it was a legal form of execution according to Canadian law or the Canadian Charter of Rights and Freedoms. No one paid much attention to the Charter of Rights and Freedoms in Canada anymore. From that time on, rights and freedoms were to be whatever the English majority decided they were.

Jacques and Simon and Pierre were dead, killed in western Quebec, and it had been only six months from the referendum. Pierre had been my very close friend, my best friend since we were young children. I cried for him, Pierre, and four years later, when you were born, I named you after him.

THE OTHER RESULT of those events was that the Canadian government decided to move the capital from Ottawa to Winnipeg. Some said that it was because that is where the new prime minister, Lloyd Axworthy, was from, but he insisted that Winnipeg was chosen because it was central to what was left of Canada. Some people in Ontario were upset. They said that the new capital should be Toronto, since that is where the real power of the country was—but if the government listened to that argument, they would have had to move the capital to Washington, D.C.

By that time, no city could claim to be the centre of Canada's economy. There wasn't much of an economy left. Cynics said the capital was moved to solve the problem of the civil service. All of the civil servants were laid off, and new employees were hired in Winnipeg—at much lower wages because the government said the cost of living was lower there. The old employees were told they could move to Winnipeg and then apply for the new jobs. Many of them didn't bother, especially the Québécois. The requirement that many employees had to be bilingual was dropped, so they were not wanted anyway. It turned out that not nearly as many civil servants were hired. Whole departments were closed down and never reopened. The government didn't have the money to run them.

ANGER TURNED TO VIOLENCE in western Quebec, and then violence turned to full-scale civil war. People fled in all directions. Towns were burned. People were killed. Within a few months, a new border had been established deep within Quebec, a border defined not by any act of government but by the progress of the fighting. It was a fluid, moving, undefined border, with people dying miles on either side of it, but it was a border nonetheless. It remains a border to this day.

5

THE NORTH was more than a direction for Canada, more than a location. It was a metaphor, a magic phrase, a defining statement. When other people thought of Canada, they thought of snow and igloos and polar bears and Inuit. Canadians liked that image, but very few of them actually wanted to live in the north. They mostly preferred the cities along Canada's southern border. Canada never really had much use for the Arctic, never did much with it.

But the north was a useful image, an illusion, a fantasy. The north defined Canada as cold and white and pure. In fact, the Canadian national anthem talked of "the true north strong and free." That was written in the 1800s, when social Darwinists believed that the white peoples in the northern part of the globe were stronger and smarter than the people who lived near the equator. They argued that people were more vigorous if they lived in a harsher, more challenging environment because there only the strongest could survive—an extension of Darwin's survival of the fittest theory. It was a racist image. And it was an illusion because it was the darker aboriginal people who lived in the true north, while the white people lived in the comfortable artificial environment of the southern Canadian cities.

Darwin, I might remind you, was English—real English from England, not one of these bastard English from Canada, and Darwinism was an example of English racism. The English always felt superior to us Québécois. It was one reason we hated them so much.

Québécois did not have any of those racist English ideas, none of those fantasies about the north. We are more intelligent and rational and realistic than the English. We saw the north for what it was—a source of power.

In the 1960s, when we Québécois began to seize control of our own nation—we called that the "Quiet Revolution"—we began to build massive hydroelectric dams in northern Quebec. There are many powerful rivers there, Pierre, that were doing no one any good, just waiting to be utilized. So we built massive dams and then shipped the power south to fuel the economy of Quebec. We also sold much power to the United States—we always liked the English in the United States better than the English in Canada or Westmount. These dams were a tribute to the vision and engineering skill of the Québécois people.

The problem, Pierre, is that though Québécois were hardier than the English, most of us did not live in the far north either. In fact, the only people living in northern Quebec were a few tribes of aboriginals, mostly called Cree. When Quebec declared itself to be a free sovereign nation, the Cree saw an opportunity. They declared that they themselves were a free sovereign nation—and claimed all of northern Quebec as their own. It was nonsense, of course. They were not a nation as we, the Québécois, are a nation—just a scattering of uncivilized nomads in a vast, empty land. Most of them didn't even have electricity in their shacks. But they were there, and they were encouraged by the Canadian government to declare their independence from Quebec. The Canadian government even gave them weapons and explosives. The English had always used aboriginals against us, going back to the 1600s when the English hired savages for a few trinkets to kill us.

The Cree declared independence on January 18, but no one noticed at first. Communications systems were already breaking down, and the news media—and everyone else—were preoccupied with events farther south. The only people who paid attention were other aboriginal people from across North America. They flocked to northern Quebec—through Canada—bringing more weapons. They saw it as an opportunity to establish a fully independent aboriginal nation for the first time in two hundred years. Most of them did not stay in the long run. There were tribal differences, and most of those other aboriginals had also become used to living in cities. They could not survive for long in the north. A number of them actually froze to death, and some died in other ways.

No one in Quebec paid much attention to the aboriginals, until February 21, when the electricity suddenly went out in western Quebec. We thought at first it might be sabotage by the English. However, Hydro Quebec officials soon traced it to a series of downed hydro towers on one of the main lines leading from the dams in the north.

As soon as it realized what was happening, the Quebec government rushed troops to guard the dams. It took them five days to get troops to all of them, and by that time the aboriginals had managed to rig an explosion that had done serious damage to one of the major dams. That was not an easy thing to do. These dams were massive structures, Pierre. It took a lot of explosive power to make a dent in them. After several ineffectual explosions, they had finally managed to blast a hole in one of the sluiceways. The dam was not destroyed completely, just rendered ineffective. It still generated some power afterward, but not very much. No, Pierre, it was never repaired. The Quebec government lacked the money and resources.

So why do we lack electric power now? Good question, Pierre. After the Quebec government troops were in control of the dams, we thought we had secured our vital power source. The aboriginals did not have enough fire power or courage to mount a frontal attack on our troops—I think. They never mounted such an attack anyway. The aboriginals, as I have said, were nomads, and they demonstrated that trait in the weeks to come. They appeared now here, now there. A shot would ring out in the woods, and one of our troops who had gotten too far from the dam or who had forgotten to keep his head down behind the defence bunkers would die. It was a cowardly way to fight a war, Pierre. Many good men died there. Among them was Philippe Batisse, another one of the twelve young leaders of Quebec. He understood the importance of hydroelectric power for the new Quebec, and he volunteered to go there to defend the dams. He was killed by an aboriginal sniper, by a bullet through the head.

Yes, the aboriginals killed many men at the dams. They also shot down helicopters, and attacked supply convoys. The north of Quebec is a vast territory, Pierre. We sent troops out to attack the aboriginals, but it was difficult. We couldn't use tanks or personnel carriers. The aboriginals simply scattered. We couldn't even spot them from the air. No battle was ever fought.

As I said, we thought we had secured our power supply when we secured control of the dams. The aboriginals soon learned, however, that they did not have to attack the dams. The power lines were a much easier target. They could blow up the bases of the towers, or cut the struts, or simply dismantle the towers bolt by bolt. Sometimes they shot out the transformers. We learned later that they used the connectors that attached the lines to the towers for target practice. Sometimes they just threw wires over the transmission lines and then let them touch the ground, shorting out the whole system. A couple of times, they started avalanches and rock slides which took out whole sections of the lines. There were thousands of miles of transmission lines, Pierre, and we couldn't guard them all. They knocked the towers and lines down faster than we could repair them.

That is why in 1999 the Quebec government withdrew the rest of our troops—most had been withdrawn by 1997—and abandoned all of the northern dams. We no longer had the money or men to guard a system that was inherently unguardable. And that is why much of the new Quebec no longer has dependable electric power.

TROOPS? You ask a good question, Pierre. At the time of the referendum, the Quebec government had no armed forces, only the Quebec police force. We had not expected to have to fight for independence. We thought it could be achieved peacefully, through a referendum and negotiations.

There were Québécois troops, of course. In fact, about 28 percent of the Canadian armed forces were from Quebec. We Québécois tended to join the armed forces because we were discriminated against in getting other jobs.

Why would the English let so many of us join the armed forces? I don't know, Pierre. It couldn't have been that they wanted to be fair. Maybe they hoped we would be killed in war, just as the English always used their lower classes as cannon fodder, and the Americans sent their black people to fight the Vietnam War. Maybe it was just that they were stupid. In any case, the Canadian armed forces were not a fighting force. They were really suited for building dykes, helping the victims of natural disasters and playing the role of peacemakers in other parts of the world. There were only about seventy thousand troops altogether. In spite of the fact that Canada had taken part in some of the major wars of the twentieth century, neither they nor we were a warrior people.

Just before the referendum, on October 26, one of the Bloc

Québécois members of Parliament, Jean-Marc Jacob, send out a fax on Monsieur Bouchard's letterhead to the military bases in Quebec, urging Québécois soldiers to leave the Canadian military and establish a Quebec army after a Yes vote. There were Québécois army officers ready to establish a command headquarters. There was a plan, not a very elaborate plan, but a plan nevertheless. It was never put into action.

That, too, was because of the size of the referendum vote. When we won by such a large margin, everyone was almost too stunned to react. It was thought that with such a large margin of victory, we could negotiate from a position of power, and it was not necessary to seize every advantage. We thought we had lots of time, and we could move slowly and get everything right. We thought that if we waited, we could get control of all of the military equipment in Quebec without fighting for it. That was our government's negotiating position, and we thought we could get it.

You have to remember, too, that the Canadian government was still paying all the troops, even the Québécois troops. Civil servants were being laid off and not being paid. Old people did not get their pensions. Schools were closing down. But the military were paid. In a time like that, when everything was turned upside down, priorities changed.

There were three armed forces bases in Quebec: Montreal, which was an army base and also a central depot where surplus ammunition and equipment were stored; Valcartier, near Quebec City, another army base; and Bagotville, north of Quebec City, which was a major airbase—in fact, most of the fleet of CF18 fighter planes were stored there—the Canadian military didn't use most of them, and they were being stored in Bagotville.

As I said, many Québécois officers were ready to leave the Canadian armed forces and create a Quebec army, but they were delayed by the size of the referendum win. They were expecting to take over the three military bases in Quebec without a shot being fired. They expected an agreement to be negotiated, and the English soldiers in Quebec would just walk away leaving all the equipment behind. So nothing was done. Well, not very much anyway. At the bases, the men began to divide into two camps, not officially, but in off hours they would gather with their own race and talk about the future. The senior officers in the two camps had also had some preliminary talks about how equipment might be divided or how the English might leave. All unofficial, of course, not

35

really negotiations, hypothetical speculation mostly.

Even when the Quebec government declared independence in late December, nothing was done about the military. In our haste, we overlooked it. It was an awkward time. Our troops were soldiers, Pierre, used to following orders, and now they were not sure whose orders to follow. How could these men, who had been trained to obey their officers, begin to choose which officers to follow? Nobody was sure, either, which side everyone else would come down on. Everyone was reluctant to take the first action, fire the first shot, for fear that they might find themselves a tiny minority in a dangerous situation.

Then came the arrest of my brother Jacques. At last, the Quebec government knew it must act. The Valcartier base was the one closest to the Quebec government, and the one we thought was most firmly committed to the nation of Quebec. On January 31, 1996, the Quebec government secretly called the senior officers it knew it could trust from all three bases together at Valcartier under the leadership of General Yvan Dumont. He was the man handpicked by the Quebec government to be head of the Quebec armed forces. From a poor Québécois family, he had joined the army at seventeen and worked his way up through the ranks, a very unusual accomplishment. The English called him Yvan the Terrible—after a Russian Czar—but he was not terrible, Pierre. He was a hero, a great soldier and a great man. Yes, Pierre, I understand why you may not think so—but he is a great man.

That meeting at Valcartier was ostensibly a supply meeting. Some of the officers took leave for a few days and didn't tell their English officers they were going to Quebec City. I say "English officers", Pierre, but some of them were traitors, Québécois who decided to remain loyal to Canada. Horrible to think, Pierre—their ancestry was French, but their hearts were English.

Treachery, Pierre. There occurred then something which shows the inherent deceitfulness of those English bastards. There were six military bases in Ontario, and more bases farther west. For some time, the Canadian government had been moving large numbers of troops to Kingston, the base closest to the Quebec border. We had spies planted throughout the military, but they never learned a thing. There was some question afterward whether Canadian military headquarters even planned the whole thing, or whether the English soldiers just began moving on their own.

Anyway, there they were, this massive army just hours down the highway from Montreal. On the night of Saturday, February 3, this whole army stole across the border in the middle of the night. When our troops in the Montreal base woke up on Sunday morning, they found they were vastly outnumbered on their own base. That helped make up the minds of those who were wavering, and only a tiny handful were brave enough to resist. They were quickly arrested or shot. You must remember, most of their officers, the men they were used to obeying, were away in Quebec City. And, the fact is, Pierre, many of the Québécois soldiers had left the base, perhaps a third of them. Some had resigned their commissions shortly after the referendum—surprisingly, the Canadian government let them go, even promised them their military pensions would continue if they left. Others just went AWOL, walked away. Some went to the base in Quebec City.

We were not wise, Pierre. Because of our slowness, we lost the base in Montreal, and all the equipment it contained. We thought that the English would take the equipment back across the border to Ontario. They didn't. They stayed at the Montreal base in force. You must remember that the Canadian government had asked municipalities in Quebec to renounce the dream of independence and choose to stay in Canada. Many of them did so, especially in western Quebec, and so the Canadian government left its army in Montreal as an occupational force.

Some more Québécois soldiers slipped away from the base. Some had been pretending to go along with the English waiting for a time to show their true sympathies. Some declared their intentions by refusing orders from English officers or trying to sabotage equipment. Others kept quiet but were detected, betrayed by their fellow soldiers, and arrested. Later, after the Bagotville massacre and The Long March to Nowhere, most were eventually shot. So that is how we lost the base in Montreal.

When the Québécois officers meeting at Valcartier heard about what had happened, they were furious. Yet, General Dumont and his colleagues were also brilliant tacticians. There are situations in war when a frontal assault is the best tactic, but this was not one of them. The Montreal base was too secure for a frontal attack, of course, but the Québécois could have attacked elsewhere. Still, they did not. They knew there was too much to lose. An open outbreak of armed conflict would have doomed the Québécois soldiers still in the Montreal base and in bases elsewhere in Canada. These men were among the few trained soldiers Quebec had, and they were needed.

But this does not mean that General Dumont did nothing. In fact, he acted very decisively. Within an hour of hearing the news from Montreal, he had arrested all of the English soldiers at the Valcartier base, and any Québécois soldiers who were known to have sympathies with the English were also arrested.

The Québécois officers then hastily assembled an armoured column to rush north and secure the base at Bagotville—you must remember that the Québécois officers from Bagotville had come to the meeting at Valcartier. By nine the next morning, they had arrived at Bagotville. They knew fifteen minutes before they arrived that they had been too late. Smoke was drifting toward them from the base.

The English had planned there too. Somehow, they had made contact with armed forces headquarters in Ottawa. Early that morning, English pilots had flown a dozen or more of the CF18s off the base, heading for Ontario. Many of the planes had been mothballed, and were not ready to fly. In the middle of the night, a handful of English officers and soldiers at the base had sabotaged those planes that they had not been able to fly out. Vital parts were missing from some. However, most they had simply blown up or set on fire. That was the smoke that was rising from the base when the Québécois column arrived. As they drove through the gates, huge explosions rocked the base, as the main storage depots blew up.

The Québécois column found the English gathered in one corner of the base, at least some of them. Some had been killed by the Québécois soldiers when they realized the enormity of what had been done. Sporadic gunfire was heard, and some fighting was going on. The Québécois column soon brought an end to that. Bagotville was primarily an air base, and there were not a lot of weapons there for fighting a land battle.

When the column had secured the base, some of the Québécois officers wanted to execute all of the bastard English. What they had done was not an act of soldiers in a war, but an act of sabotage, of terrorism, of betrayal in the deepest sense. However, Jacques de Coeur was there, and he dissuaded them.

Monsieur Bouchard had sent Jacques there as a representative of the Quebec government to help negotiate an agreement on the division of the military equipment. There was now little to negotiate. The English had seen to that. But de Coeur convinced the Québécois officers that if they took revenge now, they would endanger the lives of their own comrades in Montreal and the rest of Canada.

In the end, after five hours of difficult negotiations, de Coeur and his colleagues reached an agreement with the English. The English would be allowed to leave, without arms and without transportation, but with field backpacks containing rations. They could march all the way back to Ottawa. They marched south to Valcartier, where they were joined by those arrested there. Then they marched out of Valcartier just before sunset. Their journey was later called The Long March to Nowhere.

Jacques de Coeur served his country well. He had negotiated an agreement that would give Quebec control of all of the military equipment still left at Bagotville and that would free the Québécois soldiers in Montreal. Negotiations had been going on there too, and the English had agreed to release all of the Québécois soldiers when the English marchers from Bagotville and Valcartier reached within a hundred kilometres of the Ontario border. But they never kept their word, those bastard English. Most of the Québécois soldiers in Montreal were courtmartialled for treason. Many were executed.

As I said, Jacques de Coeur was a hero, Pierre, but he was not rewarded for his heroism or his achievements. It turned out that the departing English had boobytrapped more of the equipment than we had at first thought. There were several explosions, hours and even days after the English left. It was perhaps two weeks later. Jacques had gone with some officers to look over the equipment that remained. His head was blown off in one of the explosions. Years later, rumours surfaced that the officers had arranged to place him in the way of one of the explosions they knew were coming, or even that they had staged a final explosion for his benefit—out of revenge for him letting the English walk away—but that is just another English lie. That is the way with the English. They added slander to their treachery. And they killed another good man, Jacques de Coeur.

The column of marching English reached Valcartier, at least most of them. Two of them were killed by snipers along the march, either Québécois soldiers or civilians, I don't know. No one was ever sure afterward—but it gave people ideas.

Most of the English soldiers' wives and families had left already, in cars—many had Quebec licence plates. One supposes they made it safely to Ontario. After all, Québécois would not harm women and children. Some made it, I know—it was announced in the English press, so I suppose they all did. Many widows were present at the memorial service in Ottawa.

Widows, Pierre? Yes, the English soldiers did not fare as well as their families. They marched out of Valcartier early on the morning of February 7. They sang "O Canada" and "The Maple Leaf Forever" as they marched—the arrogant bastards! Those are evil songs, Pierre, which celebrate the capture of Quebec by the English two and a half centuries ago. But we had the last laugh, Pierre. It took us two and a half centuries, but we finally gained our independence.

And those English soldiers paid for their arrogance. At first, they marched down the highway, but late that afternoon, as they passed a wooded area, some Québécois shot at them. Maybe it was just some hunters or farmers who saw those soldiers and lost control of their emotions. You have to understand, Pierre. It had just been announced that my brother Jacques had been executed by the English earlier that morning.

The English weren't arrogant after that. They threw themselves down in the mud of the ditches and tried to hide. Brave soldiers!

A few more of them died during the night. The next day, the English switched to the backroads —and later to the woods and open country. But they were travelling blind. They were travelling through the heart of the Québécois nation, and the Québécois people rose as one to rid themselves of this evil infiltration into their very lifeblood. The local people knew the terrain, knew the best locations for ambush. Every Québécois in that area wanted to take advantage of such a splendid opportunity to gain revenge on their hated enemies. The last small group of English marchers were hacked to pieces with axes and knives and chainsaws in a little woods between the small towns of Sans Pitié and Nulle Parte.

6

"THE EAST" has always been an ambiguous term in Canada, Pierre, although it almost always had negative connotations. There was a joke in Canada that asked why the Messiah was not born in Canada. The answer was that we didn't have three wise men in the east.

I have been told that people out on the Prairies considered Ontario and Quebec to be "the East." They were always talking about how "the West" was being cheated and oppressed by "the East," that "the East" overtaxed "the West" and used the money to enrich "the East," and they hated "the East" because of it. But, how could that be, Pierre, when it was English Canada, including "the West," that was oppressing and overtaxing Quebec? Our Québécois leaders commissioned studies by economic experts which demonstrated conclusively that the Canadian government took far more money out of Quebec than it put back into Quebec in the form of services. The trouble was that some people in English Canada commissioned studies by other experts, who demonstrated conclusively that Quebec got more out of the Canadian government than it paid in taxes and that it was English Canada that was getting cheated. Who's to know? Experts can lie the same as the rest of us. The money had to be going somewhere. Maybe both sides were cheated and it was the politicians who got rich. But, judging from what has happened since, I wonder whether, financially, at least, it was more like a good marriage—both partners got more out of it than either one put in.

Anyway, Pierre, that whole definition of "the East" was wrong. We are the centre, Pierre. There was to the east of us another "East"—the four Atlantic provinces of New Brunswick, Nova Scotia, Prince Edward Island and Newfoundland. *That* was Canada's true east.

Those provinces were poor and insignificant. Their only real importance was that they had once been French long ago, back in the seventeenth century. The French there were called "Acadians." But the English overpowered them, and then drove the French out of their homes. They stole their land, and the Acadians were sent into exile in the swamps of Louisiana. That is where the English first began to practise genocide against the French. Then, after the English took over, the Atlantic provinces became poor. That is always how it is whenever the English take over. They create poverty, misery and death.

That was before the English took control of Quebec by treachery. They did not drive us away—we were too many for that or there was nowhere left to drive us—but they tried to assimilate us. For two and a half centuries, they tried to assimilate us—but they failed. We survived, and in the end we took back our land. We are now the masters of Quebec again, after two and a half centuries of oppressive occupation.

The east did not matter, Pierre, except for New Brunswick. In 1995, there were still some French in northern New Brunswick. Yes, I know they teach you nowadays that the English had eliminated French outside of Quebec, but there were still French in New Brunswick. In fact, 40 percent of the population in that province were French-speaking. Some were descendants of Acadians who had come back. Others were Québécois who had migrated there from Quebec's eastern townships. We were starting to take back our land, Pierre.

When Quebec claimed its sovereignty in the referendum of 1995, and violence broke out on Quebec's western border, not much happened on the eastern border at first. As I say, the area was poor, and the population was small. Maybe it was not worth fighting over. Or maybe it was that the English in the Atlantic provinces were too poor and weak to fight as the English in Montreal and Ontario did.

About the end of February, there were some isolated incidents of violence. Things were a bit uncomfortable for the French in the bigger towns and cities, and some began moving to Quebec. That was not what our leaders wanted, Pierre. They had more vision than that. They understood that if the English were denying the integrity of Quebec's western border, two could play at that game. In early April, our government sent Thomas Didime as a special representative to the French in northern New Brunswick. He was young, but we wanted him to appeal to the young French men and women, to the future. Thomas's argument was simple. It was that since a majority of people in northern New Brunswick were French, then the border should be moved east—northern New Brunswick should become part of the new Quebec.

Some of the older French did not want to leave Canada, for economic reasons mainly. They did not want to lose their unemployment benefits, their government medical plan and their pensions—by that time, many of those things were not being paid anyway, but they hoped that sometime in the future things would get better and the payments would resume. They were wrong.

There were some English in the area, too, and of course they did not want to become part of the new Quebec—we didn't want them anyway. They were starting to feel insecure, because they were the minority. They weren't so comfortable or arrogant when the shoe was on the other foot. We didn't care what they or the older, timid French thought anyway. By that time, people were dying by the hundreds in the west, and we were ready to take what we wanted if we had to.

That wasn't really necessary. Thomas had done a wonderful job. He had an easy manner, always willing to listen to the other side even when the opposing arguments were stupid—as they were in this case, of course. He was a good negotiator, and he had actually reached the point of determining where the new border would be, determining where the line would be drawn, which towns were most likely to want to be on either side. Not everyone agreed, of course, but it was becoming clear that the area was divided in fact, if not in theory.

Then a spark was lit, and it all went wrong. The small town of Pas Retour was in northern New Brunswick, a largely English town for some reason in a largely French area. It was an area that would certainly have been on the Quebec side of the new border. The mayor and the local RCMP detachment—those were Canadian police who supposedly policed the provinces for a fee—you can imagine how impartial they were. Anyway, in the middle of the night, the mayor and the police gathered up the English residents of the town. The English said later that they were simply trying to escape to an English area, but that was another English lie. We think perhaps they were trying to loot the town before they went, or commit one last act of violence and injustice against their French neighbours. We don't know. There were no reliable witnesses left after it was all over. What we do know for sure is that in the middle of the night, they killed twelve people, some families and young men. Shots were fired. There were woods in that area, and most men were hunters, so they had rifles. When they learned what had happened, the French got their rifles and fired back. The English had not all left yet. There was more shooting.

The English said that fires were started accidentally in the fighting or that perhaps the English started the fires as a diversion to cover their escape. In reality, they started the fires as an act of cruelty and revenge; they were trying to murder the French families sleeping in their beds. We know that, although we have no witnesses who actually saw the fires being started.

That event, Pierre, did not so much spark a fire as an idea. The next night, just after midnight on April 29, was the start of The Unquenchable Fire. It was named after the unquenchable fire of hell in the Bible, and it was an appropriate name.

It had been a warm dry spring, the trees had only begun to bud, and the woods were full of dormant trees and dry leaves. All across northern New Brunswick and into eastern Quebec, fires were lit. It was a cowardly act of destruction. The fires were started by the English. They knew that we were going to gain control of northern New Brunswick and were determined to rob us of our rightful possession. Fifty or sixty fires were started that first night, mostly near Thomas's proposed border, and along the American border. The English said later that it was the French who had started the fires in order to establish the border by force, and that the wind had then shifted to the east.

During the next two days and nights, more fires were set, many on the Quebec side of the border. There was no pattern to the fires, no organized plan, just a lot of individuals who caught the idea and initiated their own petty little acts of revenge. Some fires were also no doubt started by incendiary bombs dropped by Canadian and American warplanes. Governments were not initiators in those days, but they often picked up ideas from the people. Aboriginals also started some of the fires, no doubt.

The Americans later executed twelve French men, and two women, whom they said had started fires. But there were hundreds of fires, Pierre, and the English must have started most of them, I suppose. No one will ever know now.

There were hundreds of fires, but they came to be known as one.

Perhaps they were in reality dozens, but no one was counting. The woods were dry, as I said, and many of the firefighting crews were no longer in place. Government had largely ceased operating in many areas by that time, people had moved, fled, been killed. French firefighters would not work with the English firefighters because they said it was the English who had started the fires, and they feared the English would use the fires to lure the French into the woods so they could trap and kill them. Many of the English firefighters also refused to fight the fires. Equipment was broken and had not been repaired or replaced. Helicopters and some other equipment and crews had been moved by both French and English. They were needed on Quebec's western border.

In the first few days, people were more concerned with starting fires than putting them out. A French man's woods or house would be set on fire, so he would set fire to his English neighbour's house or woods. It is much easier to start a fire than to put one out after it has got going.

By the third day, it was too late. The winds had risen early on the second day, and the fires began to feed on themselves and each other. By the end of the third day, the whole area covering northern New Brunswick and eastern Quebec, even parts of the United States were a single blazing inferno.

People started fires and then came home to find their own houses on fire. They tried to save their homes and failed. They tried to flee, but the roads were blocked. Those who didn't die in the fires died in the smoke. It is thought that perhaps 60 percent of the people living in that whole vast area died, 100 percent in some areas. The fires raged for weeks, died out and started again.

When it was finally over, doused by the fall rains, no one worried anymore about where the border was. There was a vast, blackened wasteland there between the two nations, and it was never crossed.

Somewhere in that vast black wasteland, among all those charred unrecognizable bodies was Thomas Didime. We don't know where. He was never seen again, and those who knew where he was most probably died with him.

THE MARITIME PROVINCES were among the greatest casualties of the break-up of Canada. They were a poor backwater, disconnected from the rest of Canada. More than any other region, they had relied on the

Canadian government for financial handouts. The Canadian government wasn't handing anything out after December, 1995, and the Maritimes were in deep trouble.

Early in 1997, the Maritime provinces held a referendum of their own, and voted overwhelmingly to join the United States as the fifty-first state. It was touch and go for a while whether they would be admitted to statehood or just be a territory, but they were accepted finally, after three or four years of hesitation. A fifty-first state, many Americans felt, would upset the symmetry of the number fifty, but other Americans began dreaming of sixty or a hundred. Americans always dreamed big—almost as big as Québécois—but they have been lucky so far, and their dreams have not all come true.

The three Maritime provinces—New Brunswick, Nova Scotia and Prince Edward Island—became one state, called Atlantica. A stupid name, but nobody really cared by then. The vote was overwhelming, but the voter turnout was light, and enumeration had been haphazard. They voted Yes, but no one was very passionate either way, unlike our vote a year and a half earlier. People in the Maritimes had little hope by then. It was a marriage of convenience, more like accepting bonds of slavery than bonds of love, a desperate action taken in order to survive.

The Americans have a huge naval base in Nova Scotia now. They are drilling for oil on the continental shelf, and American trawlers from New England catch most of the fish on the Grand Banks.

There was a fourth province, Newfoundland. They voted against joining the US. It wasn't that they didn't want to be in the same country with Americans, I heard, but that they didn't want to be stuck in the same state with Nova Scotia, New Brunswick and Prince Edward Island. Like us, Newfoundlanders always wanted to have their own country, and we gave them that. I am not sure that they were grateful. Also like us, they paid a big price economically for it. I understand the Cree and other Natives took out most of their hydroelectric dams in Labrador, just as they did with ours. The people of Newfoundland said they were losing money on them anyway.

So I guess Newfoundland doesn't have much electricity now, like us. They can't have much food either. Fishing isn't worthwhile, with the Americans having pretty much fished out the Grand Banks. We don't hear much about them anymore. I think they are still there, hanging on, clinging to the bare rock for life, like us.

7

SOUTH is the opposite of North. We hated the English in Montreal and in Canada. So why, you may ask, did we like the English in the United States? It would be easy to say that we liked them because they did not oppress us, but that would not be true. It was the English in Canada who made some attempt at bilingualism, learning some French so that they could communicate with us. Maybe it was that the Americans had rebelled against England, and thus set a precedent that we could follow—over two hundred years later. We could have rebelled against England in 1776 when the Americans did, but we didn't. Perhaps that would have subjected us to a stronger and closer power, the United States, who would have assimilated us more completely. Maybe even then, not rebelling was a way of rebelling, of choosing to stay separate from the majority English culture in North America. Certainly, we were a larger minority and found it easier to survive in Canada than we would have in the United States. It set the stage for 1995, when we had grown large and powerful enough to take the next step of complete independence.

Perhaps it was inevitable. One Canadian historian said that Canada was a country created in defiance of geography. All of the geographic and natural trade routes in North America flow north-south, while Canada tried to force them to flow east-west. At times, with the Canadian Pacific Railway and the Canadian Broadcasting Corporation, it looked like they would succeed. But I suppose you can't fight geography, Pierre. That is why we lost northern Quebec.

In any case, we have always had warm feelings toward the Americans. That is why so many Québécois spent their winters in Florida, to cultivate warm feelings. Florida? Yes, Pierre, that resort state in the southern United States. Thousands of Québécois went down there to enjoy the sun every winter. There were so many of them that they even had French newspapers there. How could we afford it? No, Pierre, we did not steal rides down on trains and camp on the beaches. We drove our cars down and stayed in expensive hotels and time-share condominiums. Québécois could afford many things in those days that are unthinkable now.

Other Québécois did not go as far south. They moved down to Vermont and other northern states in order to get jobs, just as they migrated to northern Ontario and to New Brunswick. But the ones who went to the United States lost their French language. There were no French schools there, just as there are no French schools on the south shore of the St. Lawrence now.

Our Quebec politicians were always going south. They tried to encourage Americans to invest in Quebec, just as they tried to *dis*courage investment in Quebec by the Montreal English and the Ontario English. We tried to overcome one enemy by selling our future to another. Perhaps, in the end, freedom consists only in this, that we can choose our masters.

Our politicians were also trying to convince Americans that it would be a good thing if Quebec were to separate from Canada. The Americans were afraid that economic and political instability on their northern border might cause them some economic and political problems too. Perhaps they were afraid of the precedent. If French Quebec could separate from Canada, perhaps Spanish California or Puerto Rico could separate from the US. From our side, we knew that we would need American economic help if we were to survive economically after independence. I suppose we were also trying to make friends with the Americans so that they wouldn't intervene to help Canada keep us from separating. The Americans were always interfering in countries to the south of them, even invading them with armies to "protect American interests"—a pleasant phrase to cover armed invasion. In the end, I don't think our efforts were very successful. The Americans did not intervene to keep Canada together. They were more opportunistic than that.

NORTH AND SOUTH had other meanings too. In those days, people often talked of an economic north and south, the rich industrialized countries largely in the northern hemisphere and the poor developing countries largely in the southern hemisphere. Countries in the south often pointed to the unjust trading and economic practices that kept them poor. The south was demanding equality with the north.

Canada was a rich industrialized country then. We in Quebec claimed that we were oppressed, although we were not as poor as the global south. Still we always identified with the south more than with "the true north strong and free." They say you should be careful what you wish for—you might get it. We are no longer part of "the true north." We are now part of the south, economically if not geographically.

LOOKING BACK, it is surprising that it didn't happen sooner. The Americans were waiting for an occasion, a pretext, perhaps.

The American government had always said that it preferred a united Canada—for military reasons. I am not sure that that is true. If anything, I think they wanted a Canada united to the United States.

The Unquenchable Fire on the border of Quebec and New Brunswick might have furnished the excuse, but it didn't. The Americans used that, however, as an excuse to move troops into northern New England—to fight the fire, they said. And some of them did fight the fire, of course. The Americans always tell the truth, even if it is only a shield for a bigger lie.

The trigger actually belonged to an anti-tank missile. I told you that English Canadians had seized control of the military base in Montreal. They were really quite unassailable there. Their superiority in tanks and weapons prevented French Canadians from even thinking about attacking them there.

But they had to leave sometime. When they left the base, they always did it in force, because we controlled many of the streets. As I told you, significant fighting had broken out along the Ontario-Quebec border, and the Montreal base anchored the south end of the Canadian line. We soon learned that we did not need tanks to fight tanks. We could ambush tanks with anti-tank missiles and then run away on foot.

On June 17, a Québécois patrol ambushed some tanks near the St. Lawrence River. A stray shell hit an American freighter, blowing away

49

much of the superstructure, killing three men and injuring two others. That was all it took. They were all Filipino nationals, but that didn't matter. It was an American ship, and in American eyes that meant that they were Americans. It is a funny thing. If they were second-generation American citizens living in Philadelphia, they would have been considered Filipinos, but since they were on an American ship in Quebec waters, they were undoubtedly Americans.

There was a huge furore in the American Congress. On June 20, both houses approved an emergency resolution authorizing the United States "to intervene as necessary in the Quebec situation to protect lives and property." It was later alleged that the "emergency resolution" had been drafted and approved by leaders in both houses months earlier.

Neither Québécois nor English Canadians had been paying much attention to what was going on south of the border. Such neglect is always a mistake for neighbours of the United States. Troops were evidently already in place.

JUNE 24 is St. Jean Baptiste Day, a day honouring St. Jean Baptiste, the patron saint of Quebec. Every year, we ignored Canada Day, July 1—it was a hated day which commemorated our enslavement by the English bastards. Instead, we celebrated June 24 as a national holiday. You may think it strange. We no longer believed in St. Jean Baptiste, whoever he was. We no longer believed in the Roman Catholic Church or even in Christianity. But we still made use of the Day. St. Jean Baptiste was no longer a symbol of Christian faith but a symbol of our faith in the Quebec nation. We used his Day as a celebration of the Quebec nation and a declaration that we would eventually become independent.

1996 was different, because it was the first St. Jean Baptiste Day when we could celebrate the reality instead of the hope. And did we celebrate! There were parades, and concerts in the parks. People had hoarded food for weeks so that we could feast on that day. I had dinner at the home of André Roche, another of the twelve young leaders from referendum night, and the brother of your namesake, Pierre Roche. He and his girlfriend had an apartment in Montreal, and we had a roast chicken. It was a joyous time.

The celebration had actually begun the night before with huge fireworks displays—most of them fired across our western border into English territory. There were some real fireworks—they served as an effective cover for the artillery shells and mortars. Imagine it! Crowds of Canadians who had gathered to watch our fireworks were surprised when a stray rocket went off course and landed among them—and even more surprised to discover it was an anti-personnel shell—if they had time to think anything at all.

But that was the night before. The Day itself was for celebration, not for fighting. We ate. We sang. We drank heavily—to celebrate the present and to forget the evil past—perhaps to forget the evil present as well. We danced in the streets, until a heavy thunderstorm shortly before midnight drove us all indoors. By two or three o'clock in the morning, we were mostly all asleep, exhausted from our day of celebration and from drinking and eating too much. Few of us even heard the first tanks. André, who had been on the street and had taken shelter from the storm in an abandoned store—he heard. He was still carrying a two-metre Québécois flag he had been waving at the celebration.

AFTER MIDNIGHT on June 25, American tanks and troop carriers moved across the border. At three or four in the morning, they rolled through the streets of Montreal. When we woke up that morning, American troops were in control of virtually the entire south shore of the St. Lawrence River. The Americans had also seized every one of the islands of Montreal, and even Vaudreuil and Soulanges, the Quebec triangle between the Ottawa and St. Lawrence Rivers. English Canadians said they had even taken over a corner of Ontario, but I don't know about that.

In one night, the Americans had taken ownership of the largest city in Quebec, the major airport and the St. Lawrence Seaway—almost without firing a shot. You can't fight the most powerful military force in the world. A few Québécois, thinking the Americans had come to help the Canadians, fired a few shots or shouted insults. They died quickly. The Americans hadn't come to help the Canadians. They had come to help themselves.

I think probably there was so little resistance because the Americans came so suddenly and in such force that we Québécois did not realize what was happening. It took a perceptive person to grasp the situation. One of those who did was André Roche. When he saw the tanks rolling into Montreal, he knew.

The government of China is a cruel dictatorship. In 1988, there was a student movement calling for democracy, and they staged a month-long demonstration in Tiananmen Square in the capital city, Beijing. You don't challenge strong dictatorships. That protest movement was crushed by tanks. Hundreds were killed, hundreds arrested. A memorable scene from that time—a scene shown around the world on television—was of a young student standing in front of a tank, trying to keep it from advancing. The tank twisted from side to side trying to go around the young man. He kept dodging back in front of the tank, trying to slow its advance. The young man was not killed, the tank finally succeeded in going around him; he had only delayed, not stopped the advance of the tanks.

That was a memorable picture, Pierre. I remember it clearly, even now. Perhaps André remembered it, too, the night the American tanks advanced into Montreal. He stood on a bridge leading to the Island of Montreal, holding his Québécois flag. When the tanks came, he stood in front of them, waving them back with the flag, seeking to stop American military power with an idea, a declaration of justice and freedom.

The difference between China and the United States, Pierre, is that the United States is a free society, a society not bound by fear or the meaningless regulations of a cruel dictatorship. The American people are free to act in all areas of religion, morality and social practice. The driver of the first tank in the American column was not bound. He was a free man, and he rolled right over André without even slowing down. I doubt if he even felt the bump in the road. By the time the entire column had passed over André's body, there was not enough left to bury.

THE AMERICANS said they were merely safeguarding an international waterway. The implication was that they would return the land once the situation had settled down and the war between Canada and Quebec was over. Within a couple of days, there was an American fleet patrolling the St. Lawrence River. The Americans also took over the Canadian forces base in Montreal. The Canadian forces drove out on July 4. The Canadian government said the troops were needed farther north on the Quebec border. Perhaps they had known the Americans were coming. Or perhaps they knew an inevitability when they saw one. All I know is that almost twenty years have gone by, and southern Quebec is still controlled by the Americans.

That is why there is a huge American air force and navy base in Montreal now. In fact, the city has been renamed Lincoln, after the name of the base. The Americans said the name represents freedom—the base is named after the American president who brought freedom to black slaves. We remember that it was the same president who cruelly crushed the separatist southern part of the United States with military power, a man of blood and death.

The base is the largest employer in the area, and Québécois girls work as prostitutes in the bars around the base—as local girls serve around every other American military base in the world.

By the beginning of 1997, all schools in the American sector were required to teach in English. The pupils recite the Pledge of Allegiance to the American flag every morning. All signs are to be in English only, and businesses are required to use only English. It is a terrible thing, Pierre, to force people to have signs only in the majority language. Yet, this was not hard to enforce. Americans own and control all the businesses now. Some businesses were simply taken by Americans on the grounds that they had been abandoned by their owners. The American military sold them to American businesspeople for "unpaid taxes." In some other cases, Québécois (and even English) were "persuaded" to sell their businesses to Americans—often for the price of a single meal. The Americans paid in American money, which they said was exchangeable for Canadian dollars at a rate of ten thousand to one. The Americans evaluated the businesses in Canadian dollars of course, so they could claim they had paid thousands of dollars, fair market value, for the businesses.

Why didn't the people complain, Pierre? Some did, but it did no good. Southern Quebec did not become a state. It remained a "protectorate," and it remains a protectorate to this day—which means that its people have no vote and no rights, no say in what goes on. They are finally like the slaves they once claimed to be.

Some Québécois slipped across the River to the real Quebec, of course. Not as many as you might think. There was not much to go across to, by then. Some made half-hearted attempts, and then settled down to the safer course. At least, there were jobs and food in southern Quebec. But this was not what we had fought for for so many years, Pierre.

The ethnics, as you might expect, proved to be traitors. Many of them welcomed the Americans with songs and cheers. American flags appeared from nowhere in downtown Montreal, carried by the ethnics who had tried in vain to keep Quebec from her destiny.

So that is how southern Quebec was lost to us, just as western, northern and eastern Quebec have been lost.

8

I HAVE TOLD YOU many evil things, Pierre, but now I will tell you the most evil thing of all. It occurred on July 1, the most evil day in the calendar. July 1 was the day on which Canada had officially begun back in 1867. Ever since, it had been a day of national celebration in English Canada and a day of mourning in Quebec. However, it was always observed as a holiday in Quebec as well as Canada—we Québécois took that, too, as we took whatever other benefits we could get from the English—the benefits were few enough.

July 1 fell on a Monday in 1996, and the Quebec government had declared it *not* to be a holiday for people in Quebec, those who were working. We could scarcely afford holidays by then, but we did observe St. Jean Baptiste Day. The Quebec National Assembly made a point of meeting on July 1—although there was not much work for it to do—but the National Assembly wanted to show its contempt for the English Canadian holiday, and many of the members made a special effort to be there.

You remember I mentioned Judas Simon d'Estaing? He was one of the twelve young men called to Quebec City on the night of the referendum to represent the new society that was being born that night, the new nation that we were creating. I don't like to think of it now, but maybe there was a flaw in that new nation, an inherent corruption in the concept of that new society. I don't know. What I do know is that there was an evil presence among the twelve representatives of the new Quebec. Judas Simon d'Estaing was a traitor.

D'Estaing, as I have told you, had financial training, and had worked for the Bank of Montreal. After the referendum, he was asked to stay in Quebec City and help set up the Quebec government's bank accounts in branches all across our new country. These were an attempt to get those who were refusing to pay taxes to the Canadian government to pay an equivalent amount to the Quebec government in trust. That attempt largely failed, Pierre, but d'Estaing, I'm told, did a good job getting the accounts set up within forty-eight hours. His knowledge of banking was very useful.

After that, d'Estaing stayed on in Quebec City working for the national government. He was a young man with new ideas, and he was paid less money than the previous civil servants. Maybe he was an idealist, who believed in the cause. Or maybe he thought he could steal much more than the government paid anyone anyway. Those accusations were made later by General Dumont.

One thing is sure. D'Estaing had not supported Quebec nationalism in order to suffer. He believed the rhetoric that Québécois would all be wealthier, much better off in the new independent Quebec. He was one Québécois who voted with his mind as well as his heart—but maybe that says there was something fundamentally weak with his mind. I do not know.

In any case, it seems that d'Estaing must have become disillusioned in some way. Maybe it was the Americans invading southern Quebec that convinced him that the Québécois would not succeed in setting up their new nation in reality as they had envisioned it in their minds. Maybe such a nation was not possible on earth after all. Or maybe it was that he was bought off by the English. He certainly could not have done what he did without help. Afterward, thirty thousand dollars was found scattered around on the floor of his apartment—in United States money, the currency of the occupiers, of course.

The National Assembly was meeting into the evening. D'Estaing showed up at the building in a small truck, with several other men, about eight o'clock in the evening. He said he was delivering boxes of budget documents which he had had photocopied and which were needed by the finance minister, who was going to make a major announcement. D'Estaing was well known around the National Assembly, a trusted associate of the finance minister. He and his colleagues carried the boxes into the building, and around nine o'clock they left. Fifteen minutes later, the entire building blew apart in a massive explosion. The entire cabinet, our leaders who had achieved for us the dream of a sovereign nation, died. Some Members of the National Assembly survived—they had been in other parts of the building or had left early or were elsewhere doing other things.

No one ever learned the identity of d'Estaing's fellow assassins. The English later claimed that they were Quebec soldiers—a terrible lie, Pierre—the English were not there, so how could they know a thing like that? Most likely they were Canadians. They were certainly English. Whoever they were, they escaped, probably across the bridge to the south shore controlled by the United States. D'Estaing had been paid in US dollars, remember.

D'Estaing? No, he did not escape, Pierre. They found him the next day, hanging from the balcony of his apartment. He had hung himself. He himself had pronounced judgement on his betrayal, his unspeakable infamy.

Why did he do it? How could he betray his nation like that? No one knows. He left a hand-written suicide note of sorts, in his pocket. It said only, "It was not what I had expected," and he had signed it. Not what he had expected! That was no excuse! The way things turned out was not what any of us had expected. That does not justify killing innocent people and attempting to bring an end to a nation.

It was an attempt to bring an end to the Quebec nation, Pierre. Of that I am sure. Maybe d'Estaing hoped that, with our leaders dead, we Québécois would give up and submit again to the English. If so, he was wrong, Pierre. Well, if you wish to know the truth, Pierre, all of it, the good and the bad....the National Assembly was not really in control of much by then anyway. They were politicians, Pierre, used to fighting political battles for the minds of people. They were ill equipped to handle the situation we had found ourselves in for most of the past year. They had tried to change history by passing laws, but laws do not control history, Pierre; they only reflect it.

JUDAS Simon d'Estaing's body was cut down by soldiers of General Dumont. Then the General had his body taken out to a place near the old city called "the Plains of Abraham." It was where the English had defeated a noble French army in 1759 and gained control of Quebec. It was where our servitude had begun two and a half centuries earlier. And there General Dumont determined to bring our servitude to an end.

He had d'Estaing's body taken to that field, in front of the television cameras, with the world watching—the American TV networks had film crews present. General Dumont had d'Estaing's body fed into a wood chipper and sprayed all over the field. The chipper had been left there months earlier by a work crew who had been interrupted by the revolution—I mean, the referendum, although I suppose it is true to say that it was a revolution too. D'Estaing's body was ground into tiny pieces and sprayed over the field. There was nothing left to bury. The pieces were eaten by birds and small animals and dogs. It was an act of supreme contempt for the English and their temporary victory on that field. It was an act of defiance, a declaration that the Québécois people would never again be subject to the hated English, the despicable English, no matter how many atrocities they committed. That is why the name of that field was changed to the "Field of Blood," the name that you know it by today.

General Dumont then made his famous "Vive le Québec libre" speech, from a platform erected on the field, surrounded by Québécois troops and other citizens. He said that never in the history of the world had such a deed been contemplated by any so-called civilized people, to try to still the voice of a people by blowing up their national assembly.

Oh, Pierre, what a question! Sometimes I am almost ashamed to call you my son. Yes, your namesake, Pierre Roche, and some other Québécois, had been accused of trying to blow up the Canadian Parliament—but that is just groundless speculation. Here you had an actual deed. Actual people dying. Besides, such an act, if it had been true, would have been justified, a just revenge for the way the English had mistreated our people all those years. I do not want to talk about that, Pierre. That is not the important thing.

That speech, Pierre, it was magnificent. Next to the referendum night, it was the greatest day of my life. In a few simple words, General Dumont summed up the aspirations of the Quebec people. He reminded his hearers that another General—General de Gaulle of France, had voiced those same aspirations in Montreal in 1967, on the hundredth anniversary of the founding of that insidious instrument of oppression, Canada. Now, he, General Dumont, would repeat those words, not as an aspiration, but as a declaration of fact, "Vive le Québec libre." Quebec lives, and she lives as only a true nation can live—free.

THE NEXT DAY, work began on rebuilding the National Assembly building. It wasn't on as grand a scale, and in fact it still has not been completed—it is just a shell where ceremonial meetings are held. But it was a symbol, a symbol of our will to survive as a nation. We live by symbols, Pierre, and General Dumont understands that.

The government went on, perhaps even more efficiently than before. As I told you, some of the Members of the National Assembly had survived the attack. A few of the former Bloc Québécois members had never taken up their seats in the National Assembly when they had been given them after the referendum. Some senior civil servants were appointed to fill the places of the cabinet ministers who had been killed. You remember how the law had been changed allowing such appointments? The leading army generals were also appointed to the National Assembly. It made sense, given the state of war we were in. It was a popular move, another symbol of our resolve to fight on for our freedom as a nation.

General Dumont himself was given the title "Protector of the Québécois People." He was our protector in a very real sense, head of the army that protected us from the attacks of the hated English. It was General Dumont who ran things after that. Out of the chaos, he brought order. He is still doing that, Pierre, almost twenty years after the referendum. He is still our leader, the only national leader you have ever known. We must be grateful to him, Pierre—he is a great leader. Don't ever say otherwise. It would not be prudent; the walls have ears.

ONE OF THE FIRST THINGS General Dumont did next was to organize our forces along the Ontario border. What had been a chaos of violence shifting back and forth over many thousands of hectares of land, he placed on a military footing. All the Québécois men in western Quebec were drafted into the army and organized into commando units to attack the English. It was our revenge for the outrage of the bombing of the National Assembly.

That was the beginning of the national draft, which continues to this day. It is an important part of the Québécois character, Pierre. When they turn sixteen, all Québécois men and women are drafted into the army for five years of voluntary service. They are not paid, of course. It is a voluntary service. They are trained to defend our nation. They also do many other things to serve our nation—build roads and bridges, help out in disasters, work in mines and on the collective farms. Most important, it is a time when they are taught to be completely committed to serving our nation and to obeying General Dumont as the leader of that nation. Then, after five years, some choose to stay in the army and be paid, or to leave the army and do other work, if they can find it.

Yes, Pierre, I understand your sixteenth birthday is approaching and you must leave soon. I understand why you do not want to personally be drafted into the army—even though the punishments and conditions there are not as bad as the rumours that run wild among you young people. I understand, and I do not blame you. But the idea, Pierre, the glorious idea of serving the Québécois nation—that, Pierre, is a noble, glorious vision.

That vision was justified by the results of that first experiment with it along Quebec's western border. As a result of General Dumont's initiative, we made real progress. We began to push the English out of Quebec. The English later said that our commando units mainly slaughtered women and children, and sometimes Québécois men who would not join the army. English lies, Pierre. What really was happening was that we were winning the war. General Dumont was a military genius. That is why the English called in the United Nations to protect them. If they had not done that, we would soon have driven the English out of Quebec, and probably reclaimed our rightful land in northern Ontario too.

The cost? Well, sure, some of our troops were killed in the escalation of fighting, but not very many. Well, people were dying anyway. Whatever the cost, we paid it willingly. We were willing to do whatever General Dumont told us in those days. Oh, of course, we still are, Pierre, we still are. I would not suggest otherwise.

THE UNITED NATIONS? As I said, Pierre, we Québécois and the English were fighting a vicious war along Quebec's western border. The English became desperate and committed many atrocities. They have accused us of committing atrocities too, but we, Pierre, have been merely trying to defend ourselves from attack. Our atrocities, if there have been any, have been truly defensive atrocities.

After the Americans moved into southern Quebec and then the National Assembly was blown up, the level of violence increased greatly. On July 24, the Americans called for an emergency meeting of the United Nations Security Council. By the end of the week, the Security Council decided to send peacekeeping troops to Quebec's western border. They arrived early in August. There were no Canadians or Québécois available, of course, so the troops were largely Swedes, Norwegians and Germans—with a few Americans thrown in, so everyone would remember who was giving the orders.

After that, the fighting gradually died down. The situation became what it is today—with only the occasional sniping or lobbing of artillery shells across the border, followed by negotiations, then a lull for a few months, and then a little more shelling.

NATHAN THOMSON was, as I told you, another one of the twelve young leaders. As you might guess from his name, he had some English ancestry, but he was a Québécois through and through. He was also a very gentle man, a man with a pure heart; he hated no one.

Before 1995, Canada had gained a reputation as a peacekeeping nation, and troops from Quebec had played a great part in that. Whenever there was a war or a civil war, Canadian troops were asked to go in as peacemakers. They would establish themselves between the fighting parties and try to keep them from killing each other. It was a task that required great tact, wisdom and diplomacy on the part of Canadian and Québécois soldiers. They had served in many countries over half a century, and they had earned much praise for their efforts. In fact, they were once awarded the Nobel Peace Prize for their work.

No one was prouder of this effort than Nathan Thomson. He had several relatives who had been in the Canadian armed forces. He had even asked Lucien Bouchard to let him set up a task force to determine how Quebec troops could carry on this peacekeeping tradition after Quebec became a separate country.

Nathan was a very sensitive man. When he saw United Nations peacekeeping troops marching up the Ottawa Valley to take up their positions between fighting Canadians and Québécois—well, something snapped. I think it broke his heart. On August 6, he got hold of a Canadian army rifle and walked out onto the middle of a bridge over a small river that marked the new border. No one saw where he had come from—they decided afterward that he must have crawled up to the bridge under cover of some trees. Anyway, he was on the bridge before anyone saw him. He stood there for ten minutes, looking at the Canadian fighters on one side of the river and then the Québécois fighters on the other side of the river, and the UN soldiers standing guard at either end of the bridge. And then he put the barrel of the army rifle into his mouth and blew his brains out.

He was the second last to die, and he died of despair.

Two of the twelve young men representing Quebec's future committed suicide, Pierre—one committed to Quebec and the other paid by Canada. Perhaps they symbolize our two nations committing themselves to a path that leads to death. Or perhaps they were only two weak men who could not keep their commitments.

9

ON OCTOBER 30, 1996, General Dumont ordered national celebrations to mark the first anniversary of Quebec's declaration of sovereignty. A year had passed, and we had achieved the status of an independent nation, and we had maintained that independence in the face of military, economic and political opposition. It was a cause for great rejoicing, and General Dumont ordered that we rejoice. There were huge parades, mostly consisting of marching soldiers.

Important speeches were made in every town praising General Dumont's achievements. He was called the father of the Quebec nation, the one who had achieved independence for the Québécois people. It was announced that day that Quebec City had been renamed Dumont in his honour, an announcement that brought applause, Pierre. It was inconvenient to have the capital and the country carry the same name. Moreover, it clarified that General Dumont represented the government in his own person—he was the government.

It was also announced that from then on, October 30 was to be a national holiday, the premier holiday in the nation of Quebec. Workers were given the day off—without pay, of course. It was time to sit back and ponder what we had achieved.

IN 1759, when the English conquered Quebec and our long nightmare began, we were a tiny nation of sixty thousand scattered along the St. Lawrence River. In the over two centuries of our captivity, like God's chosen people in Egypt, we multiplied and prospered in spite of our slavemasters. The Roman Catholic Church wanted to keep us as we were in 1759—poor illiterate farmers scattered along the St. Lawrence River—but we threw off those chains, as we later threw off the chains of the English. We were greater than that, and we could not be kept from our destiny.

By the time of the referendum, in 1995, there were over seven million people living in Quebec, about 82 percent of them Québécois. A survey taken before the referendum, in March, 1995, showed that between half a million and a million people would leave Quebec if Quebec separated from Canada. We would be glad about that; it would purge our great nation of the rich English in Montreal and the ethnics. We would be stronger as a result of their departure.

We do not take censuses in Quebec anymore, Pierre. That is what the English used to do, and we are not English. The English took censuses so they could brag about their numbers and use the numbers to oppress us. It also did not seem a priority when there were so many other things that needed to be done. A census would cost our government money that is needed for other things.

Still, we can estimate, Pierre. There are well over a million free Québécois now, more than twenty times our number in 1759. We live in our own sovereign nation spread all along the north shore of the St. Lawrence River, and our settled territory extends about twice as far north of the river as it did in 1759. We have truly conquered, achieved our destiny as a free and prosperous nation.

YES, PIERRE, my story is drawing to a close. I will quickly tell you the rest. There is not much more to tell.

On Referendum Day in 1995, the twelve of us were called to Quebec City to stand around Monsieur Bouchard and Monsieur Parizeau, twelve young men representing the new holy nation of Quebec. We were not called to Quebec City on October 30, 1996. Nine of us had died, and it would have been too sad altogether for a festive occasion like that. We were not even there. Well, Matthieu Levis was there, but he was not asked to stand behind General Dumont. The General appeared on the platform and on television surrounded by army officers.

You remember that Matthieu had been in the Canadian tax department, and had financial expertise? After the death of Judas d'Estaing, Matthieu was given his position in the finance department.

He served faithfully in that position, and was even promoted twice. He became quite a powerful man.

Where is he now, Pierre? Well, the short answer is he was caught in the Millennium Purge. You remember, after a few years of independence, there was considerable unrest in the Quebec nation. The economy was doing poorly, and some people had begun to lose faith in the new Quebec. On January 1 in the year 2000, the dawn of the new millennium, army officers suddenly arrested several hundred important leaders and civil servants in the Quebec government. Those in charge of the economy and financial affairs were natural targets because of their mismanagement of the economy.

General Dumont solemnly informed the nation that those arrested had been plotting to overthrow him as rightful leader of the new Quebec. It was rank ingratitude, after all he had done and sacrificed for Quebec, after he almost singlehandedly had achieved freedom for our people.

Matthieu Levis was arrested with the others. Specifically he was charged with stealing money from the government accounts in an effort to bring about the collapse of the Quebec nation. You understand that I do not know myself the truth of those charges, but General Dumont declared them to be true, and he would not lie. I accept his word, Pierre.

Jacques Petit told me that he had received a letter smuggled to him by a mutual friend. The letter was not signed, but he recognized Matthieu's handwriting. The letter said that Matthieu had not been paid in some time, and that he was thinking of doing something desperate, stealing small amounts of money from the government accounts in order to keep his two-year-old daughter from starving. He asked Jacques to take care of his daughter if anything should happen to him.

Matthieu was tried by the Military Protectorate Court and found guilty of treason. He was shot by a firing squad on the Field of Blood outside Quebec City in February, along with one hundred eighty-eight others. Drastic action, Pierre, but necessary to protect our nation and its beloved leader, General Dumont, from treason. Those executions were a useful warning to others who might try to disagree with the General and thwart the will of the Quebec people. There have been no major coup attempts since that time.

Jacques Petit did not go to take care of Matthieu's daughter. It would not have been wise. Jacques lacked the means to care for her in any case. I understand General Dumont took care of the girl.

YES, PIERRE, that left only two of the twelve apostles of the new Quebec. After the events of 1996, both Jacques Petit and I retired from active politics. There were not many civil service jobs anyway, and many of the good ones went to army officers.

That is when I moved here, to this small town of Patmos. I took up a vacant farm, and I (or I should say we) have managed to grow enough food to survive. I met your mother here. We lived together for two years. She died the night you were born. She had not had a proper diet during the pregnancy, there were shortages, and the birth did not go well, there was no doctor available....You are her gift to me, Pierre. It amazes me still that you survived. And you will survive still. You are Québécois. You are wise. You will do what Québécois have always done—find a way to survive. If that meant we must lay down our lives to achieve the status of an independent nation, we would do that. And if that now means that you must leave Quebec, so be it. I understand, as our people have always understood.

YES, YES, I will tell you about Jacques Petit too. Early in 1997, about the time I moved here to Patmos, Jacques moved to another small town, Desespoir. He did not choose as wisely as I. The soil was not as good there, there was no good vacant land. He was not a practical man, Pierre, a scholar more than a labourer. He managed to put together a cabin, a shelter of some sort, in the woods. He wrote me a letter once, saying how strange it was that there were only two of us left. He worked at odd jobs sometimes, and some people gave him food when they had any to spare. It was not enough. He lasted five years, perhaps more than could be expected. In the spring of 2001, someone found his body lying on his bed in his cabin. No autopsy was done, of course—we don't do those things now—but he had apparently starved to death.

It is sad, Pierre. Monsieur Bouchard said that the twelve of us represented hope, the future of the new Quebec. Only twenty years have gone by since that night, yet I, Jean Tonnerre, am the only one left. After you go, I will live out my days here in Patmos, alone, like an exiled prophet.

AND YOU WILL LEAVE, TOO, Pierre. I understand that. There is little for you here now. But there is little for you to go to in Canada either. Things may be better there than here, but not much.

Canada, too, is now a military dictatorship. Democracy was no longer necessary for us once we had independence. Democracy and voting are English inventions anyway, Pierre, a tool that enabled the English majority to oppress the Québécois minority. I suppose in that sense democracy is no longer necessary in Canada either. In Canada's case, military dictatorship was imposed to control looting and crime, to maintain law and order. The English were always big on law and order, as long as it was English law and English order. And democracy no longer works very well when you have a desperate lower class with nothing to lose. Such a class cannot be made to obey laws and governments—except by force.

Canada has such a lower class now, just as we do. Well, what do you expect with unemployment over 30 percent and governments bankrupt? Medicare, free medical care for all citizens, was abolished in Canada in 1996. It was a temporary measure intended to preserve scarce medical resources for the war effort, but like so many other temporary measures it has become permanent. Most of the doctors in Canada and Quebec have moved to the US to make more money anyway. Unemployment insurance was made self-funding in Canada in early 1996, with payments geared to contributions. By 1997 the payments were so low, no one bothered to apply for them anymore. Welfare payments were abolished the same year. There are some privately run food banks, but government has little money. What economy there is is mostly underground. The barter system is common.

Some trade in raw materials is still carried on from British Columbia and Alberta, I understand, but Canadian manufacturing scarcely exists anymore.

In the spring of 1997, the United States took "protective custody" of "an important international waterway"—the Northwest Passage—just as the US had taken control of the St. Lawrence Seaway earlier, and as the US took "protective custody" of the West Coast salmon fishery in 1997. In effect. "protective custody" of the Northwest Passage meant that the US took possession of all of Canada north of the 60th parallel and added it to the state of Alaska, including all of the mineral rights. Oil drilling has become a major operation in the region, with only one or two significant oil spills. The Americans know how to do things right.

That is why there will be a referendum in Canada next month to decide whether the people there want to join the United States. One wonders only why it took so long. I suspect it would have happened sooner if the Americans had been willing to let the Canadian provinces come in as US states. They will join as a protectorate now, so the US does not have to give Canadians full rights as citizens. Otherwise, the US would have to provide social security and other benefits to Canadians, and that would be too expensive.

It is all window dressing, Pierre. Personally, I think the English planned it all along. Look at what will happen. The English in all of North America will now all be united under one government. Quebec will be an even smaller French island in an even bigger and more unified English sea than was the case in 1995 when we voted to preserve the Quebec nation. The future looks precarious for Quebec now. Some American senators are already hinting that we Québécois need to be protected from the aboriginal threat on our northern border. The Americans are not a tolerant people, Pierre. It is a dangerous thing to come under their protection. Considering the way they have treated black slaves in the past, and Hispanics in California, and remembering the way the Americans have treated Québécois in the occupied parts of southern Quebec, well, I am afraid, Pierre. As a minority culture, you can only withstand the pressure of a great empire for so long.

10

THE CANADIAN DOLLAR was called in English a "loonie," Pierre. It was a coin with a gold colour but was not made of gold. It looked more valuable than it was. The coin was called "loonie" by English Canadians as a term of derision, since no one liked the coins, which were awkward and inconvenient to carry.

We laughed at the Canadian dollar, but fundamentally the Canadian economy was sound. In Quebec, the Canadian dollar represented economic strength. In our hearts we wanted our own independent country, but in our minds we knew that we needed to be connected to Canada to prosper economically. Our Quebec governments always complained that the Canadian government took more out of Quebec in taxes than it put back in in services. It was a dubious claim, Pierre, but the larger the numbers, the easier it is to diddle with them. It was also an irrelevant argument. All along, our leaders knew that economically we needed English Canada, that together both countries were stronger than we would be if we were completely separate. We wanted independence with our hearts but economic union with Canada with our minds. We wanted a separate Québécois culture in a Canadian economy.

Our Québécois leaders knew this, Pierre, that we wanted to eat our cake and have it too. So, they devised a mixed recipe. We never called for "separation" from Canada. We talked of "sovereignty association"; "sovereignty" represented cultural independence, and "association" represented economic cooperation. We talked of this contradiction in such rational language that we never suspected that it might be irrational, that the methods required to achieve "sovereignty" might make "association" all but impossible. That is also why the Quebec government kept defining referendum questions calling for sovereignty association or "a new economic and political partnership." They were a deliberate appeal to the ambiguity of the Quebec nation.

In the 1995 referendum, we asked Québécois to vote "Oui" to sovereignty association, to a new economic and political partnership with Canada. It was a big advantage to us the way the question was phrased, much better than asking Québécois to vote No to remaining part of Canada. It forced our opponents to argue for a No vote, to be negative. It is always harder to get people to vote for a negative option.

The huge billboards we erected throughout Quebec featured the one word "Oui" in huge letters, but we replaced the "O" in "Oui" with a Canadian dollar, a loonie. This meant that people could vote for our side with both their hearts and their heads. To vote no would be to vote against the Canadian dollar and all the economic prosperity that it represented.

It was wise planning, Pierre. It is an axiom of politics that if your position is weak in one area, you should stress that area. The more bold the lie, the more it will leave people shocked and unable to reply. If your immorality becomes an issue, campaign on how you will restore morality to politics and the country. If your economic policies have caused economic ruin, campaign on how only your economic experience is capable of solving the economic crisis. It takes away your opponents' best argument. It may not convince people, but it will confuse them, which is almost as good. No, Pierre, it is not manipulation, only an application of the God factor.

Looking back, it is very ironic, Pierre, how we stressed the Canadian dollar in 1995. In order to reassure those who were hesitant, we insisted that Quebec would continue to use the Canadian dollar even after separation—the English could not stop us from using any currency we liked.

We were wrong, Pierre. In September of 1995, the Canadian dollar was trading for about 74 cents in United States money. Economists said that that was considerably below its real value. The economists, who were English, said that this was because Quebec might separate from Canada and investors don't like uncertainty. This was absurd. The leaders of Quebec kept going to New York and Washington to reassure investors that nothing would change economically if Quebec became a free nation. Those foolish English investors didn't believe the Québécois leaders. They said that no one could predict what would happen. They were fools.

In early October 1995, when the violence started and it began to seem likely that Québécois would vote Yes, the dollar began to fall. Two weeks before the referendum, it dropped below 70 cents US, an unheard-of level. A panic had set in.

After the referendum, the Canadian dollar dropped even further. It hovered just above the 60-cent mark until November 13, when Simon Levis announced that he would no longer pay taxes to the Canadian government. At that point, fears set in that the Canadian government might not be able to pay its bills. The dollar dropped to 50 cents. Those fears became reality after November 27, when the Canadian government stopped making payments to Québécois. By early December, the Canadian dollar had dropped below 40 cents US. The Canadian government stopped making payments on its foreign debt in December. It had lost over 20 percent of its tax base in losing Quebec, and the economy was in trouble in other parts of the country. By the time the violence began in February, the Canadian dollar was worth only about 10 cents. By the summer of 1996, the Canadian government was printing money like crazy in order to pay soldiers and government employees. The last time anyone paid any attention, the Canadian dollar was worth only a cent or two US. Now, like Québécois, Canadians use US dollars. The Canadian government still issues some Canadian money, but no one pays much attention except coin collectors.

It is ironic. We had campaigned on keeping the Canadian dollar, but within eight months, the Canadian dollar was worthless.

There was irony in Canada, too. Many people in Alberta and other parts of western Canada had assumed that they were so far away that it wouldn't make any difference to them if Quebec separated. It soon became obvious that they had been wrong. The English media were full of stories of companies that were benefitting from the low Canadian dollar and exporting more products. The reality was that unemployment was rising rapidly. Businesses in Montreal were moving out or closing up. Businesses in English Canada that had sold products into Quebec, cut back or went broke altogether. The Canadian government was cutting payments for welfare and pensions and unemployment benefits. Civil servants were let go. The Canadian government sent less in transfer payments to the provinces, and the provinces, already facing lower tax revenue, began laying off teachers and nurses and civil servants. The burning of the forests in New Brunswick, and the civil war along the Quebec-Ontario border destroyed real wealth. Because of the uncertainty, no one was rebuilding. Unemployment quickly approached 25 percent of the workforce. Later on, it exceeded it. Now no one even has meaningful statistics.

In theory, a low Canadian dollar should have had Canadian export businesses thriving. In fact, when the dollar reached the 50 cent mark, the US government essentially cancelled the North American Free Trade Agreement by enforcing "anti-dumping" provisions, and Canadian exports almost stopped. Companies in Canada and Quebec couldn't get raw materials, production equipment, computers or government subsidies. The Canadian and Quebec economies collapsed, along with the dollar.

SO, IF WE NEEDED CANADA to survive economically, why didn't we just stay part of Canada? Why was it necessary to separate to protect our culture? You are right, Pierre, but you are also wrong. We had survived for two centuries as a distinct society within Canada. But we had lived poor and isolated, in small villages and on farms. Even the industrial revolution did not change that. We continued to live in the same small towns and work in local pulp mills and asbestos mines. It didn't matter what language people spoke in Ottawa or Toronto or New York or even Montreal. We could still speak and live in French.

But we couldn't survive the information revolution. After the Second World War, in the 1950s and 1960s, everything changed, Pierre. The English wouldn't leave us alone. They bombarded us with radio and movies and, worst of all, television—all in English. They invaded our homes. And the English changed the economy so that there were no jobs in rural areas and we had to move to the city where it would be easier for them to make us English.

After we moved to the city, we also abandoned the Roman Catholic Church, which had told us to remain on the farm and in the local factories, and thus kept us poor. And when we abandoned the Church, we adopted birth control. Our population began to decline.

That is why we had to become active in politics to protect our culture. We had survived for two hundred years, but our nation was now in deadly peril. We tried to fix the problem, to save the Québécois language and culture, by passing laws. We passed laws saying that stores could not have English signs outside, and inside any English signs had to be much smaller than French signs. We also passed laws forcing most people in Quebec to send their children to French schools. We even gained some control of immigration so that we could bring in French-speaking immigrants instead of English-speaking immigrants.

Why did the English let us do this, Pierre? That is a good question you ask. I don't know. Perhaps they were just foolish. More likely it was because we threatened them. They were afraid we would separate if they tried to stop us. We used that fear whenever we needed to. They complained, and they challenged the laws in court, but they were afraid of us, Pierre.

But culture is more than language, Pierre. It is a shared history, common patterns of thought. That is why bringing in French-speaking immigrants from Haiti and other places and forcing people to go to school and to shop in French did not work. The Haitians did not vote for separation any more than the other "ethnics." The French language and the Québécois culture were being swamped in a sea of English. We could not have survived if we had stayed in Canada.

So we created our own country to preserve what was left of our language and culture. We concluded that our enemy was the Canadian government, that if we could just remove the power of the Canadian government from our lives, then the French language and Québécois culture would be saved.

Perhaps it was too late, for I am not entirely sure that we have succeeded in preserving our language and culture even now. When I think about it, I sometimes wonder if we miscalculated. After all, it was the Canadian government that provided civil service jobs in French, that provided French-language service in airports and post offices all across Canada, that forced companies to put French on the labels of the goods in stores in Quebec and all across Canada, that provided French radio and television, and cultural grants to Québécois artists and singers and academics. All of these French-language services provided jobs for Québécois. Because of the Canadian government, we could leave Quebec and travel and do business in French in the rest of Canada.

I am beginning to think, Pierre, that the enemy of culture is not government but culture. We could get rid of the Canadian government. We could not so easily get rid of the social and economic forces of the

English. Just as lines on a map are invisible on the real earth, so social and economic forces are insidious. They laugh at borders.

In the end, we learned English for the same reason the Chinese and Japanese and Europeans learned English—because business is conducted in English, because jobs are done in English, because the movies we wanted to see were in English, because the best computers were programmed in English, because the most powerful nation in the world spoke English.

You do not hear much discussion of whether signs in stores in Quebec should be in French or English now. By 1997 the language laws were no longer enforced. We had to have signs in English in order to attract American tourists. We were desperate for employment and cash infusions of any kind. And you don't see French packaging on what goods remain on the shelves in stores in Quebec either. I think companies would consider bilingual packaging for a Canadian market of thirty million people, but not for an impoverished market of one or two million. We can no longer afford to make movies and music CDs in French. If we ever try to leave Quebec for jobs or business ventures—well, when you leave Quebec now, Pierre, you will find no services or jobs in French out there. You will have to work and live in English. We created our own country to save our Québécois culture, but now I wonder whether that may only have hastened the loss of that culture.

I suppose our mistake was not that we were foolish to think that the Canadian government could destroy Québécois culture, or that a Quebec government could save it. It was more than that. It was our foolish pride that we could be in control of anything, even ourselves. Our mistake was in thinking that, like God, we could do anything we wanted. The international markets soon disabused us of that notion.

WE USED THE ANALOGY of a family. We told Canadians that Quebec was like a child who had grown up happily in the Canadian family but who had now reached maturity. Quebec had been protected in that family but had also been denied responsibility. Now it was time for that child to go off on his own and be independent. What we envisaged was a transition that was natural, healthy and inevitable, with the warm family relationship remaining intact afterward.

We were a prisoner of our own analogy. Perhaps the analogy was not valid. In many ways, Quebec was not like a child. We had a say in

74

what went on. We had had freedom, rights, responsibility. For most of the last three decades of Canada's existence, a Québécois had been prime minister.

Perhaps a family analogy was valid, but a different analogy. Perhaps Canada was like a husband who was patronizing and controlling but generally decent and indulgent to his wife—even though he did not understand her. Quebec in turn was like a slowly maturing wife unsure of what she wanted. She continually used blackmail and the threat of going home to mother to get her husband to give her more jewellery—without ever making up her mind whether what she really wanted was the jewellery or to go home to mother. She stayed with her husband without ever committing herself to him. Perhaps what we really wanted was not to go or stay but to have power, the power to choose.

The usual outcome of such a relationship is obvious. Perhaps it is just as well that we won the referendum in 1995. To have voted No would have just meant more years of uncertainty. We would have kept on having referendums until one time the circumstances were right, the economy was stagnant enough, we had been offended sufficiently by some family quarrel....The irony in such cases is that the wife does not consciously choose to go any more than she chooses to stay. The sad thing is that while some of us had finally achieved our dream of independence, other Québécois were no more committed to being part of an independent Quebec than we had been committed to being part of Canada. It is sad to say, Pierre, but Quebec was a nation with a divided soul, and separation has not changed that.

You grew up without a mother, Pierre. I did not. But two years before I went off to university, my parents divorced. My father, your grandfather, divorced his wife, my mother, your grandmother. Did you know that? They were both dead before you were old enough to know them. Theirs was not a terrible marriage, but like Quebec and Canada they had drifted apart. While the divorce was being processed, my father told his lawyer to arrange an amicable settlement. He said that he wanted to be considerate and generous to my mother, adding, "I want to remain friends afterward." The lawyer laughed. "Don't be a fool," he said. "Couples are never friends after a divorce."

WE HAD ENVISIONED a quiet, rational and friendly divorce from Canada, to be followed by an economic partnership, but it was not possible, Pierre.

The trouble is….See, there was some discrimination and racial tension. There were clear cases where we had suffered injustice at the hands of the English. And we did think of ourselves as Québécois first, not as Canadians. Even the man we called a traitor, Prime Minister Pierre Trudeau, had been a Québécois in his heart. He worked hard to keep Quebec part of Canada, but he didn't care a fig for English Canada. He cared about Quebec and believed that remaining part of Canada was the best thing for Quebec. So you see there were good reasons for Quebec to separate, to become an independent country. But you can't base a revolutionary change on a good idea. You have to build passion, a sense of outrage, in order to make people change. We did that, Pierre.

If truth be told, Pierre, I sometimes think that English Canadians had not treated us all that badly when compared to the racial oppression that occurs in other parts of the world. We called ourselves "the white Niggers of America," comparing ourselves to the blacks in the United States, who were first dragged to that country as slaves and then, after slavery was abolished, treated as second-class citizens. They were given inferior schools; they had to sit in the back of buses; they were not allowed to hold certain jobs or associate with white people; they were not allowed to vote. Some of them were threatened, beaten, raped and killed—and when they objected, they were denied justice because the white people controlled the police and the courts. Sometimes things like that happened to us, but not as often. We were allowed to vote, and often we held the balance of power in the Canadian Parliament—we portrayed English Canada as a united force ganging up on us, but English Canada was often divided, and we used that to our advantage. I tell you this, the United States would have been a far different place if the Democratic Party had had a tradition of alternating between white and black presidential candidates and of nominating a black candidate for vice-president whenever it nominated a white candidate for president. That is what the Liberal Party did with Québécois.

Because of this situation, we had to make use of what injustice there was. We used isolated incidents. We used statistics. Decisions and choices are made all the time by governments, agencies and companies. Whenever an English person or company was chosen over a Québécois person or company, we claimed discrimination. The Canadian government could not always choose a Québécois, so of course there were always plenty of incidents to tell people about. We used these incidents to force governments and agencies and companies to choose Québécois more often, and when they didn't, we used those incidents to show the injustice and discrimination we suffered at the hands of the English. But it wasn't only us. The governments of the English provinces played the same game for selfish political motives. No, no, Pierre, it was not dishonest, just an application of the God factor.

SO, I AM AFRAID that our dream of an easy, friendly and rational separation from Canada was just that—a dream, totally divorced from any reality. Canada had a worldwide reputation for tolerance, for compromise, for peacekeeping. Canadians were famous for stopping wars, not making them. The Canadian armed forces were a joke, underfunded and undermanned. Someone once described the Canadian military as "the people to send in the moment the fighting stops."

So, you understand that we Québécois were quite confident that Canadians would never fight to keep Quebec part of Canada. It never entered our heads. So who could have predicted that separation would lead to so much fighting, so many deaths? Who could have predicted that our actions would result in so much hate? Who could have predicted that both Quebec and Canada would today be military dictatorships?

HOW DID IT HAPPEN? I said before that you young people are not taught history any more. At least, you are not taught history from other parts of the world—only Quebec's is thought useful. Perhaps you should have studied Russian history, for instance, or even the history of the French Revolution. History demonstrates that moderates who start revolutions are usually quickly replaced by more extreme men and women and that revolutions almost always result in military dictatorships as oppressive and brutal as (or worse than) the governments they displace.

We had said that Canadians would never go to war to keep Quebec part of Canada. Canadians were not like Americans, who believed their nation was divinely ordained, who worshipped "one nation under God." Americans had a military history and would go to war to keep their country together. But Canadians had a long history of compromise and conciliation and peacekeeping and would not go to war to keep their country united.

We were right. Canadians did not go to war to keep Quebec from separating. But we were also wrong. There was a civil war. Canadians were not willing to fight to force Quebec to say in Canada, but they apparently were willing to fight over a long list of other things—over the division of government debt, over the division of government assets, over the St. Lawrence Seaway, on behalf of the Québécois who wanted to remain part of Canada, out of anger because we had torn apart their country.

HATRED, PIERRE. It is a dangerous thing to incite racial hatred for political reasons—or hatred of any kind. In order to build up the passion necessary to bring about separation, we had to point out all the negatives about Canada and stress all the injustices. We had to build a sense of outrage and anger. The problem was that that strategy created anger among the English as well as among Québécois. And once we had filled people with anger and hate, it was impossible to keep them from acting on it, with fists and guns as well as ballots. Once we had taught people to hate, once so many of us and them had suffered and died, it was impossible to put the genie back into the bottle. It was impossible to tell people to stop hating and go back to cooperating. Societies operate by trust, and once trust had been destroyed, it could not be restored overnight.

We had said that we would negotiate a new economic agreement with Canada after separation. It was logical and would have benefitted both sides. But I have discovered that people don't live by logic, Pierre. We proved that when we voted Yes in the referendum. Looking back, it should not have been surprising that the English refused to make an agreement with us after we had called them racists and oppressors and destroyed their country. But we were surprised, Pierre, and that shows you how badly we had miscalculated.

THERE IS something else. You have heard about democracy, Pierre. It means that all of the people have a say in what happens, a right to freely discuss the issues, a right to vote for what they want. That is what we did in the referendum. We discussed the issues and then we voted.

Yes, I know that we do not seem to have that now. In the first few years after independence, elections were postponed until we could regain all of our land and all the Québécois could vote. You can't hold an election in the middle of a war. Yes, I agree. We have not regained our land and are not likely to now, twenty years later, so why don't we have elections? The answer is simple. As General Dumont has explained, now that independence has been achieved, what is there left for Québécois to vote on? Our Quebec government embodies the will of the people, so what need is there to bother with elections?

It seems, Pierre, that democracy is a fragile flower. We thought it was a rock and all we had to do was say we believed in it. But words do not speak as loud as actions, and somehow in the rush to battle, the flower was crushed by soldiers' feet.

WHAT IS democracy anyway, Pierre? Making decisions by voting can be nothing more than the tyranny of the majority—and remember that in Canada we were a minority.

In the referendum, we said that democracy was everything, that a vote of 50 percent plus one would decide everything. But we forgot about the more fundamental concepts of law, legitimacy and consensus which underlie democracy and every other form of government. We thought that democracy, a simple vote in a referendum, could make the Canadian government illegitimate and just as quickly legitimize a sovereign Quebec government. We found it was much easier to destroy than to build. A new legitimacy has to be built up over the course of decades and centuries by the forces of consensus.

The Bible is an old book of wisdom revered by Jews and Christians. We don't read it much anymore in the new Quebec, but it contains an interesting story about an old king named Saul and a new king named David. Saul was old and unpopular and corrupt, and he knew that David had been chosen by God to replace him as king—but he refused to accept God's decision and tried to kill David. David lived for several years as a fugitive, pursued by Saul's army in the wilderness, but he was a great warrior and several times he had an opportunity to kill Saul. Yet each time, even though he knew he was destined to be king, he refused to kill King Saul. Finally when a man came to David and said that he had killed King Saul, David had him executed as a traitor and a murderer. David at first seems to have been a fool to pass up so many opportunities to achieve his dream of becoming king. But David was a very wise man. He did not so much refuse to kill Saul as he refused to kill the king. He knew that by demonstrating that it was acceptable to kill King Saul, he would also be demonstrating that it would be acceptable to kill King David. In preserving Saul's life and throne, he saved his own. Although there were some attempted rebellions, he ruled a long time and died in peace as an old man.

In the early 1990s, the Canadian prime minister, Brian Mulroney, was hated and despised by most Canadians—he had the support of only eight percent of Canadians in public opinion polls. Yet Canadians allowed him to remain prime minister until his term legally expired. Perhaps Canadians had read the Bible and remembered the story of David and Saul. Maybe they knew the importance of law. Or maybe they were just too apathetic to rebel. If so, there was wisdom in their apathy.

It is too bad that we did not read the Bible more in 1995. Then perhaps we would have understood the precedent we were setting. It is possible to change borders and governments by law and consensus, but it happens very rarely and must be handled very carefully. It must be done in such a way that everyone recognizes the change as legitimate. It would have been possible for Quebec to separate from Canada without violence, but it would have had to have been legally and by consensus, by convincing both Quebec and the English to agree to it.

We were not that careful, Pierre. We carelessly eliminated the authority of the Canadian government, not realizing that that act also threatened the legitimacy of the Quebec government we wanted to put in its place. That is why the rule of law is more important than democracy. Once you reject or question the authority of a government, you inevitably bring into question the authority of all governments, as well as the laws they make. If the maker of laws can be discarded at will, why not the laws themselves? Once you have broken one law, what sense of morality is there to keep you and others from breaking other laws? What restrains people from violence and evil is not democracy but law and legitimacy. I am afraid we demonstrated that when we began stealing flags to burn and began using violence in street battles against the English. Simon Levis demonstrated it very clearly when he refused to pay taxes to the Canadian government, and others followed his example by refusing to pay taxes to all governments.

We demonstrated it also by changing the borders of Canada. For once you have moved one border, who are you to say that other people cannot change other borders—and in ways not to your liking? We had insisted that the boundaries of Quebec were inviolable and non-negotiable, but once we had discarded the government and laws which had established those borders, the borders blew away like smoke. In the end, there were no negotiations, but the boundaries of Quebec changed nevertheless. Our new boundaries were established not by law but by force and by forces over which we had virtually no control.

Human laws are imperfect, and human justice systems are imperfect, but they are necessary approximations of the underlying law of a moral universe. This is important to understand, for when law ceases to be an impartial arbiter between humans and becomes a tool of competing forces, then justice is lost altogether. Once the police and the military had stopped enforcing the law impartially and begun using their position to promote either Quebec separation or Canadian unity, then they ceased to represent the Law and in fact came to represent lawlessness—as happened in the pre-referendum riot in Montreal. It is true what they said in the Middle Ages, hundreds of years before the founding of Quebec: Kings sometimes make laws, but laws always make kings.

Someone—probably one of the English—said a danger signal had come about twenty years before the referendum, when René Lévesque, a Quebec premier and one of the early Separatist leaders, ran over someone—probably an Englishman—in his car. Some people said that Monsieur Lévesque had been drinking and was not wearing glasses as required by his driver's license, but he was cleared of all charges. After all, you couldn't put our nation's hero and leader in prison—it would threaten the government and destabilize society. I don't know the truth about that incident; it happened a long time ago. And it was no worse than many of the things done by other politicians in the Canadian government and the English provincial governments. Maybe that incident just seemed unjust to the English. But I have learned that laws are more important than lawmakers, and justice more important than justices of the peace.

I also know—by experience—that it is not a good thing when the rule of law breaks down altogether. That explains the necessity for the strict rule that General Dumont has been forced to impose in the new Quebec—and which Canadian governments have imposed on Canada.

The rule of law is as fragile a flower as democracy, Pierre, and we should have treated it with more care. Or it is like a dry stone wall fitted together—if one piece is pulled out of the middle, the whole wall comes crashing down. What has been erected carefully over centuries can be demolished in a day.

Once we demonstrated that it was good to kill some enemy of another race or state, then why not other enemies? That is why soldiers

81

and police and governments are subject to grave temptation. If you have the power to make law, you may forget that you yourself are subject to a higher law, natural justice, or God's law, as we would have said in the old days. That is why crime rates have soared in both Quebec and Canada since separation. When people no longer believe in the rule of law, they have to be kept in line by terror.

THAT IS ONLY one side of the matter, Pierre. The other was tolerance. In Canada and Quebec after separation, there was an increase in crime, but there was also a decrease in tolerance, and that is also something that we had not expected. Attitudes hardened, and we were no longer willing to forgive.

Before we separated from it, Canada was not a naturally tolerant place. I don't think Canadians and Québécois were inherently good any more than any other people in the world are good. Yet, even though it was not perfect, Canada was known as a relatively tolerant and peaceful society.

I think the difference, Pierre, was that the existence of Quebec in Canada was what a friend of mine called "an involuntary anti-racist program." This goes back to the very beginning. In Quebec, the English conquerors were vastly outnumbered by the Québécois they had defeated. As a result, they knew that in order to maintain control they would have to give the Québécois language and religious rights that the English had not given to conquered minorities anywhere else in the world. This policy was proved right when the Québécois did not join the United States in rebelling against England in 1776, and so the English continued it. Even after so many English immigrants came that the English became the majority, we Québécois were still a big enough minority that they had to treat us with some consideration. Perhaps it was just habit by then. Canada was so small in population and so vast in territory that it was very vulnerable. Forced to develop east-west means of transportation and communication in order to resist the pull of the United States in the south, Canada could not afford to have a separate Quebec disrupt the St. Lawrence Seaway, the Canadian Pacific Railway or the Trans-Canada Highway. Canada was forced to placate us. I am not saying Canadians did it perfectly or even willingly—we still had ample grounds to justify separation—but, grudgingly and imperfectly, they still did it.

Moreover, what Canadians gave to Québécois, they were forced to give to other minorities. What the English called "the French fact" forced Canada to be tolerant. In order to make English-French bilingualism acceptable to the other minorities, the Canadian government created a Department of Multiculturalism and gave grants and set up human rights tribunals to protect other ethnic minorities. Again it was done imperfectly, but, like the dog that sings, one marvels not that it is done well but that it is done at all. Multiculturalism was a colossal act of folly. Billions of tax dollars were wasted on ethnic "cultural centres" that no one cared about except a few old immigrants who remembered the "old country." But multiculturalism was a symbol and a teaching tool of the fact that Canada had decided to be a tolerant society.

It was an unusual but not unprecedented accident of history. Decisions were made that Canada would be a more or less tolerant society. I am not just talking about decisions by governments or courts or human rights tribunals. (I think in the long run the human rights tribunals, with their lack of judicial safeguards, their lack of common sense and their use of force to impose foolish decisions sometimes created more resentment than tolerance—inquisitions are the enemy of tolerance, and imposed tolerance in actions can often reinforce intolerance in the heart.)

No, the decisions I am talking about were not decisions made by courts or governments. What I am talking about is the billions of decisions made by millions of ordinary Canadians and Québécois that if we were to survive and prosper, we would have to find some way to get along. It was not self-sacrificing love so much as enlightened self-interest, but it was socially useful.

When we were together as one country, we were forced, almost against our wills, to be tolerant, to make allowances. Afterward, neither society had a compelling reason to be as tolerant, as open. Tolerance was another of those fragile flowers that we took for granted. We did not choose or expect to be less tolerant, but we were.

Well, what do you think? In our new nation defined by race and culture, how could we tolerate deviation? Any deviation was a threat to the purity of our race and culture and thus a threat to our nation, our reason for being.

Remember, I mentioned that old book called the Bible? It tells the story of the Jews, who had once been slaves in Egypt. After they were freed, God reminded them of that and then told them that they were to

83

treat foreigners in their own country differently. They were to give the foreigners rights and fair treatment. We Québécois had also been slaves to another nation, those bastard English. We had felt oppression, so you might think we would have some sympathy for other minorities. We did not. The parts of Quebec that remained in our hands after 1996 were mostly the racially pure areas. It was a harsh time, and when we had an opportunity, we took our revenge on Haitian refugees and rich Jews, as well as any English that remained.

The same thing happened in Canada. The bilingualism and multiculturalism and human rights budgets were among the first to be cut when the Canadian government began making so many changes in November and December, 1995. Human rights laws and provisions were temporarily suspended so that they would not stop the Canadian government from cutting services to Québécois. Capital punishment was temporarily reimposed so the Canadian government could execute Québécois like my friend Pierre Roche. But once these things had been changed, they were never changed back.

The people we called "English" in Canada had by this time become a bastard race from many nations. They could not create a racially and culturally pure nation as we Québécois could. But it was no longer socially acceptable to have dark skin or to practise different social customs. For instance, there were a group of people from India called "Sikhs" whose religion said that they must always wear turbans and carry small knives called "kirpans." The Canadian government had even allowed Sikh policemen to wear turbans instead of police hats. No more. Sikhs no longer wear turbans in public, and many of their temples have been burned. Those who set the fires have never been caught.

Tolerance is a frail flower and it could not survive in a land bitterly divided along racial lines.

11

THE GOD FACTOR? I have explained everything else, and I can explain that, too, Pierre, but it's a little complicated.

Let me begin by saying that everyone believes in something—some higher power or some person, idea or goal that gives meaning and purpose in life—even if it is only Charles Darwin's survival of the fittest or Larry Flynt's lust.

Who was our God? What did we believe in? From the founding of Quebec as a fur trading colony, the government of France had sent us Roman Catholic priests. They weren't always accepted by the Québécois because they interfered with trade and did not want us to have relations with the Native women. Yes, strange ideas, Pierre, but that is how it is with religion, any religion—it wants to take over all of life.

The priests persisted, even brought their religion to the Natives. We didn't always listen. We could always go off into the bush or just not go to church. But then the English came. They let us speak French in Quebec, but they closed off the west, filled up the empty spaces with bastard English. The fur trade ended, and we were trapped in Quebec, like an island in a sea of English. We were trapped with the priests, and for the most part, at least outwardly, we accepted their religion. They gave us an identity as Roman Catholics, as Catholic Québécois farmers. We believed in the Christian God and let our lives be governed by the rituals of the priests, from baptism to the last rites.

The priests told us to stay on the farms so we would be influenced by them and not by the English. They also insisted that we continue to speak French so we wouldn't be influenced by the English. And they told us to have big families—I told you, religion tends to want to control everything, even sex. They called it "la guerre des bébés."[4] We had lost the war to the English, but we would have our revenge through the cradle. We would outnumber the English bastards by procreation. And we did, too—in Quebec certainly. We would have gone farther. We moved into northern Ontario, northern New Brunswick, northern New England. We reproduced faster than the English. Still, they cheated, like the English always do. They brought in more English from Great Britain. And they brought in Ukrainians and Poles and Italians and taught them to speak English, and they swamped us. Outside Quebec and even in Montreal, they swamped us. But in Quebec itself, we won the war of the cradle. We won, survived and grew numerous.

In the two centuries after the defeat on the Plains of Abraham, the Roman Catholic Church helped the Québécois people. Its influence allowed us to survive, to become strong and grow in numbers. In giving us an identity as French Catholic farmers, the Church created our sense of nationhood, it defined us as a people with a religious purpose. The Christian idea of the sacredness of human life and the Bible's command to "be fruitful and multiply"—these ideas helped the Quebec nation to survive and grow. The priests created our sense of being a nation called Québécois and then appealed to that nationalism. The priests used Quebec nationalism to build loyal followers of the church, and—here is the other side, Pierre—we used the church to build the Quebec nation. The Roman Catholic Church made us strong, but we used that strength to break away from the Church. Out of a handful of poor, conquered farmers clinging to the north shore of the St. Lawrence River, the Church created the Québécois people—but we rebelled against our creator. The Church should have known what was coming because the Church knew the Bible story of what had happened to the people the Christian God had created in the Garden of Eden.

The problem was that in urging us to stay on the farms and grow in numbers, the Roman Catholic Church also condemned us to be poor and uneducated. The priests understood the power of culture and

---

[4] "The war of babies" or "revenge of the cradle."

economics and social forces when we did not.

Finally, in the 1960s, we rebelled—it was called the Quiet Revolution. Forced to leave the farms and villages to find jobs in the city, we left Roman Catholicism behind as well. It had helped us, but now it was holding us back. We began to go to universities—and universities controlled by government, not the Church. We began to not only work in the factories, but also to own them and run them. We began to live together as men and women without our sex lives being blessed by the Catholic Church, and we began to use birth control so that we were no longer so numerous or so poor.

We did well. But there was a problem. I said before that everyone needs to believe in something, to have some higher goal that brings meaning and purpose to life. After we no longer believed in Roman Catholicism, there was a hole, a vacuum, and we had to fill it with something.

I told you before that we, the twelve young men, representatives of the new Quebec, were devoted followers of Monsieur Bouchard and Monsieur Parizeau, and later of General Dumont. We had considered these men to be our Messiahs, the leaders we had been waiting for. They would throw off the iron rule of our oppressors and make us an independent nation again. Well, all right, Pierre, it may be technically true that we had never been fully independent, but we had always been independent in our hearts.

No, Pierre, we did not worship Monsieur Bouchard or Monsieur Parizeau or even General Dumont—although we have come closer to worshipping him. No, they were only our God's representatives. It was not Monsieur Bouchard who would lead us to have our Promised Land. It was sovereignty itself which was our Messiah. The Roman Catholic God was replaced by a new god. We had rejected the Roman Catholic priests' definition of religion, but we kept the sense of purpose, the vision of our nation that went with it. We had taken the periphery and made it the centre. We had taken some ornamental brickwork of the building and made it the foundation.

Pierre, you may well ask why we did not step back. When it became obvious that independence was leading us to violence, war and poverty, why did we not stop and rethink our course? Why did we not retreat and go back to being part of Canada again? Don't you understand, Pierre? We could not. For many of us, the creation of an independent country called Quebec was not just a wise and reasonable choice. It was the choice of our hearts. Being Québécois was what gave us meaning in life; it was who we were. We were not human beings, children of God, husbands, fathers, lovers, teachers or missionaries. We were Québécois. We worshipped a God named Quebec. If we were to give up our dream of an independent Quebec, we would no longer have had any reason for living; we would have had no purpose.

What is that you say, Pierre? You think that seems an inadequate concept of divinity? It seems odd to you that we would worship imperfect human beings, who were, in fact, ourselves? Ah, but you never saw Quebec at the height of her power and prosperity in 1995. And our god is at least as good as the English gods of money, sex and power.

It is said that we become like the gods we worship. So, wouldn't making Quebec our god be the surest way to ensure that we would become what we worshipped, our own independent nation? Was there anything wrong with worshipping Quebec as our highest good, Pierre? It was a noble vision, far greater than our individual selves. But there were costs, of course. I told you before that any religion tends to take over all aspects of life. Take morality, for instance. Fundamentally, law is based on morality—but what is morality based on? It is based on religion, one's fundamental beliefs. Now, listen. Our god is defined by race and a common experience of historical injustice. So, if Quebec is our god, then morality must be whatever promotes Quebec. If our god is ethnically defined, then so must our morality be ethnically defined. What is moral, what is right or wrong, is determined by what furthers the cause of Quebec. Under such a god, everything becomes permissible—deceit, violence, hatred. So you see there was nothing wrong with spreading misinformation, stuffing ballot boxes, attacking the No headquarters after the referendum in 1995, killing....That was the significance of the God factor, Pierre.

Perhaps it is like that with all true nations—and perhaps that is why Canada has never been much of a nation. Canada is not a god. It is a pragmatic compromise, a means to an end, a tool. No one could worship that. Canadians could not bring themselves to worship such a laughable god characterized by historical accident and compromise. Perhaps that is why they worshipped sex and money—but those gods proved no better than our god—they certainly have very little money now.

Some Canadians said that it was a good thing that they didn't worship their country, but I don't know. If you don't worship your country, what can you worship?

I tell you this, Pierre. I think we were right to reject Roman Catholicism. It was often little more than meaningless ritual. It kept us poor and uneducated and on the farm. But I have sometimes wondered, Pierre, if there might perhaps be something in the idea of the Christian God, a God who is perfect and completely powerful, all-seeing, loving, just and truthful. That would be a God worth worshipping. Could such a God possibly exist, Pierre?

Does it matter that our god's values are pride, anger, revenge and racial exclusivity? What is wrong with a god who can neither achieve nor impose traditional Christian morality? Can't such a society as ours prosper if we all agree on these basic values? Would it really have made any difference if we had worshipped a God of truth, love and justice, for instance, a God of self-sacrificing love and mercy?

WELL, we had rejected all the mumbo-jumbo of the priests, all that prattle that people are infected by evil at a deep level. We believed in the goodness and saneness of human beings. We thought we could change gods, and morality would continue as before. We thought we were naturally good, truthful, loving and peaceful. Yet once the restraints of law and habit were removed, we soon discovered the evil that was in our hearts—Canadians as well as Québécois. Who would have thought that we Québécois and Canadians were capable of such hatred, violence and cruelty? That has made me wonder if perhaps the Christians' Bible might not be correct after all. It has an unflattering view of humanity. It says that we were created in the image of God, but that by our own wilfulness we rejected God our Creator, and in rejecting the good God, we made ourselves evil. We remade ourselves in our own image, and that mortal image turned rotten.

We thought we were good people, but, looking at the events of 1995-96, I have sometimes wondered if we were not horribly, tragically wrong. Well, that may have been a delusion, Pierre, but it is a delusion we share with virtually every other nation on earth—the delusion of our own goodness, importance and grandeur.

DECISIONS AND CHOICES matter, Pierre, although it may not always seem so. We had insisted that the borders of Quebec were inviolable and non-negotiable, but in the end the borders and the future of the new Quebec were determined by social and economic forces over which we had virtually no control. But that does not mean that we didn't have the freedom to choose.

The referendum in 1995 was a choice certainly, but only one. No, I don't mean separation and independence were our only option. I don't mean we couldn't have chosen differently then. We did have a choice. No, I mean that the referendum was only one of many choices. We live by choices, dozens, hundreds, thousands of choices we make every day, big decisions and little decisions, big decisions that turn out not to have mattered, and little decisions that alter the course of history—we don't always know, but we live by decisions, and we have to live with the consequences of those decisions. We made many choices in 1995 and 1996, but choices have consequences, and we could not choose to change the consequences of our choices. It seems that we could not change the fundamental laws and principles of the universe. Perhaps this is even more reason why it does matter what god we choose to believe in, even more reason why our choices do matter.

No, Pierre, the separation of Quebec from Canada was not evil. Yet I think that maybe it was an opportunity for all of the evil that we had tolerated in ourselves to come out—pride, selfishness, anger, fear, little dishonesties, the rejection of God, or at least of any God other than ourselves. All of that—well, it was not so much unleashed by the referendum as it was that we were finally able to see the results of all those things. The work had already been done, the choices already made. Our destiny was determined not so much by the way we voted on referendum day in 1995 but by all the other decisions we made beforehand and afterward.

Was it all inevitable? Was it our destiny to become an independent nation—and to suffer the consequences? No, we could have changed our course in a million ways at a million forks in the road. There are a million ways things could have turned out. Our destiny was determined by the choices we made—just as your future, our future from now on, will be determined by the choices we and the people around us make.

12

WHAT'S THAT YOU SAY, Pierre? Yes, you are right. It has been diverting to play mind games in our conversation, to build speculative fantasies with words. But, whatever truth there may have been in the words, this is just a story. It did not happen. Why not? Perhaps because we did not choose it. Or perhaps because of the grace of God. It did not happen. But it would be good for you to ponder why it did not happen—and to ensure that it does not.

www.ingramcontent.com/pod-product-compliance
Lightning Source LLC
Chambersburg PA
CBHW072153020426
42334CB00018B/1987